FORBIDDEN MANIPULATION

The Covert code to influence Anyone's Mind using NLP, Dark Psychology and Subliminal Persuasion in an undetected way – the best techniques to Analyze and control people

By Jack Hill

Edition 2019

© Copyright 2019 by – All rights reserved

This document is geared towards providing exact and reliable information in regards to the topic and issue covered. The publication is sold with the idea that the publisher is not required to render accounting, officially permitted, or otherwise, qualified services. If advice is necessary legal or professional, a practiced individual in the profession should be ordered.

From a Declaration of Principles which was accepted and approved equally by a Committee of the American Bar Association and a Committee of Publishers and Associations.

In no way is it legal to reproduce, duplicate or transmit any part of this document in either electronic means or in oriented format. Recording of this publication is strictly prohibited and any storage of this document is not allowed unless with written permission from the publisher. All rights reserved.

The information provided herein is stated to be truthful and consistent, in that any liability, in terms of inattention or otherwise, by any usage or abuse of any policies, processes, or directions contained within is the solitary and utter responsibility of the recipient reader. Under no circumstances will any legal responsibility or blame be held against the publisher for any reparation, damages, or monetary loss due to the information herein, either directly or indirectly.

Respective authors own all copyrights not held by the publisher.

The information herein is offered for informational purposes solely and is universal as so. The presentation of the information is without a contract or any type of guarantee assurance.

The trademarks that are used are without any consent and the publication of the trademark is without permission or backing by the trademark owner. All trademarks and brands within this book are for clarifying purposes and are owned by the owners themselves, not affiliated to with this document.

Disclaimer

The content of this book has been checked and compiled with great care. For the completeness, correctness and topicality of the contents however no guarantee or guarantee can be taken over. The content of this book represents the personal experience and opinion of the author and is for entertainment purposes only. The content should not be confused with medical help. There will be no legal responsibility or liability for damages resulting from counterproductive exercise or errors by the reader. No guarantee can be given for success. The author, therefore, assumes no responsibility for the non-achievement of the goals described in the book.

TABLE OF CONTENTS

DISCLAIMER 3
INTRODUCTION – WHAT IS FORBIDDEN MANIPULATION? 5
DEFINE YOUR DESIRES: OUTCOME AND GOAL 13
MANIPULATE THE MIND THROUGH NLP 17
WHAT IS DARK PSYCHOLOGY AND HOW TO USE IT? 23
MIND CONTROL TECHNIqUES 33
THE BEST TECHNIqUES TO SPEED READING AND ANALYSE ANYONE 69
THE MOST EFFECTIVE TECHNIqUES TO USE EMOTIONAL MANIPULATION, AT WORK, IN A RELATIONSHIP AND IN LIFE IN GENERAL 101
HOW TO USE MANIPULATION TO SEDUCTION 115
DEFINE AND OPTIMIZE YOUR MESSAGES, ALTERS THEIR PERCEPTION 123
LEARN HOW TO OVERCOME MANIPULATION AND USE IT AGAINST THIS TYPE OF PEOPLE 141
HOW TO USE SUBLIMINAL MESSAGES TO PERSUADE PEOPLE IN AN UNDETECTED WAY ... 148
CONCLUSION 158

INTRODUCTION – WHAT IS FORBIDDEN MANIPULATION?

Manipulation refers to the set of techniques that make it possible to modify the attitudes or behaviors of a person, independently of his will.

There are two main types of manipulation techniques:

- Techniques based on persuasion: they are exercised directly on the attitudes or personality of people.
- Behavioral technologies: they can extort behaviors that people would not spontaneously emit.

Classic persuasive techniques

These techniques are often seen in the fields of sales and marketing, but also in everyday life. They allow modeling the attitude of others. Also, a classic technique is to force sympathy to create empathy with the target of manipulation. This maneuver is rendered all the more indispensable as the initial attitude of the target is far from that recommended by the manipulator.

To understand this phenomenon, we must refer to the

model of Richard Petty and John Cacioppo, developed in 1986. These authors consider that the persuasive message is treated along two routes:

- The central route: it represents the strictly informational contribution of the message.
- The peripheral road: it represents the more informal characteristics that are systematically attached to this message.

The sympathy with the transmitter is one of those characteristics. If a receiver is not convinced by the informational content of the message, the manipulation will consist in forcing a peripheral treatment by raising the sympathy to increase the chances of adhesion.

Social proof corresponds to a technique that builds on the achievements of research on social influence. It describes an irrepressible and automatic tendency to validate a choice or an idea from the observation of the behavior of the mass. In manipulative practices, social proof is exploited in different forms. It can serve as a selling point for a product, which is then presented as highly prized. It is operative in the manipulations that consist in creating artificial queues at the entrance of the discotheques. It also explains the use of slap or prerecorded laughter to guide the public's judgment.

The principle of scarcity refers to the individual's

response to a feeling of loss of control over their environment. Thus, if an individual learns that a coveted object is becoming scarce to the point of threatening its attainment, the phenomenon of reactance likely leads him to desire it even more and to acquire it so as to restore his sense of control. Scarcity will therefore often be highlighted to force a purchase decision.

Coercive persuasion

This form of persuasion is also called mental manipulation. It can be observed in more extreme social contexts. It is used by totalitarian organizations (for example, sects) as a weapon to completely assimilate a person into an ideological system, erasing their identity.

It is then a question of limiting, or even eliminating, the interactions between the individual and his former environment. Simultaneously, the organization introduces new rules involving all of the home ranges. Thus, the individual is taken care of as a whole. Subsequently, the organization seeks to reduce the vigilance of members who may become aware of the arbitrariness of these new rules. In this perspective, it is possible that it asserts many messages of propaganda, whose purpose is to saturate the information channels. Indeed, it is in this way that any critical spirit can be annihilated.

Behavioral technologies

The theoretical basis of these techniques is due to Charles Kiesler. In 1971, this author proposed the first version of the psychology of commitment. Its purpose is to study the circumstances under which an individual is engaged (and not engaged) in his actions.

In terms of handling, we can mention different techniques:

- **The feeling of freedom:** this is the most important determinant. Indeed, an individual is all the more engaged in his act that he has the feeling of having freely chosen. Also, the manipulation techniques based on this theory all ensure the preservation of the target's sense of freedom in order to extort costly behaviors. These methods are formidable because the objectively manipulated person has the impression that his integrity of thought is respected.

- **The technique of the foot-in-the-door:** it consists first of all in obtaining from the manipulated person an innocuous behavior, called preparatory behavior. For example, an experiment consisted of affixing a sticker on a person's car to a road safety sticker. And a few days later, this person was subjected to a much more expensive request than the previous one. The results showed that this method greatly increases the acceptance rate of the expensive query. The person initially engaged in a freely determined behavior is closely related to it. This is the reason why this initial decision is reiterated on the occasion of more expensive behavioral choices centered on the same attitudinal object (for example road safety).

• **The priming technique:** it does not differ fundamentally from that of foot-in-the-door, but concerns more directly an important principle of manipulative practices. It is the perseverance of the decision activity. It consists of hiring a person by making him make a decision whose real consequences are hidden from him, always annoying for her, but advantageous for the manipulator. It turns out that a person informed of the facts after making a decision on false bases may maintain it. This technique can be observed both daily (between friends) and in sales practices, where a first decision will be extorted on the basis of a lie concerning the price or quality of the product.

• **The door-to-nose technique:** it occupies a special place because it can not be conceptualized by the theory of commitment. Unlike the foot-in-the-door, it is for the manipulator to make an exorbitant request in relation to the possibilities of the target, which will systematically refuse. However, this simple formulation makes it possible to increase the chances of acceptance of a second request, comparatively much less expensive, but sufficiently problematic not to have to be accepted spontaneously.

What is Mind Control?

When the term mind control fails, many people initially think of brainwashing. Perhaps even an unclear, mystical process that can not be precisely defined. In fact, the term refers to a specific set of methods and techniques, such as hypnosis or thought-stopping, for influencing a person's thoughts, feelings, and actions.

Mind control techniques are not inherently evil. When mind control techniques are used to give someone more choice but retain decision-making power over their lives, it can have a very positive impact. So people have quit smoking with the help of hypnosis. However, when mind control is used to change the belief and value system of an individual without his knowledge and consent, and to make the subject dependent on external authority figures, it can have devastating effects.

Destructive mind control aims to destroy nothing less than a single identity - behavior, thoughts, feelings - and replace it with the idea of the leader/group. This is done by strictly controlling the physical, spiritual, emotional and spiritual life of the devotee. The uniqueness and creativity of a person are suppressed.

Consciousness control practiced by sects is a social process that encourages obedience, dependence, and consensus, and is often compounded solely by the size of the group. It is achieved by immersing a person in a social environment in which they can function only if they discard their old identity and accept the new one desired by the group.

Individuals are exposed to co-ordinated psychological and social processes with the aim of effecting attitudinal and behavioral changes and maximizing control over members' lives.

This proverbial mental programming is not a one-time process but a gradual process of destabilization and transformation. He can be compared to the weight gain, first a few grams, then half a kilo, finally a kilo. Without even noticing the first change, you suddenly have a different shape.

So to mind control. Turn here, push there - and there we have it: a new inner attitude, a new point of view. It is a concentrated effort to change a person's world view, their consciousness, which also changes their behavior so that the person does not notice their own change.

Anything that might reinforce the old self-image is pushed aside and replaced by the reality of the group. Independence and individuality are discouraged. The free choice is pushed back in order to undermine the freedom of choice of the individual.

The person assumes a totalitarian ideology that, once internalized, replaces its former value system. Often there is a radical change in personality and a complete break with the previous life. This process can be activated within a few hours, but it usually takes several days or weeks for it to stabilize.

The beliefs of the group become the only concern of the person. Anyone who does not fit into this newly formed reality becomes irrelevant. Totalitarian groups make their members practically addicts.

DEFINE YOUR DESIRES: OUTCOME AND GOAL

How to slip your ideas into people's mind

Everyone has seen the movie "Inception," right? How they can secretly plant ideas into people's mind, that would be amazing, wouldn't it? Just for a moment, imagine you could really do that. You could slip ideas into other people's minds. What ideas would you put there?

"Buy my product." "Give me your phone number." "That's a great idea!"

But that's fiction, right? Not really. The truth there is really is a way to get people to think the way you want them to. Of course, you should never abuse this. You should always make sure that the ideas you are getting other people to think are things they want to do anyway, right?

Abusing of this power it's not a good idea, not just for moral or ethical reasons. Because if you do, people are going to know, and they are going to be very angry. Therefore don't do it!

That being said, how do you use this wonderful technique of covert hypnosis?

Simple, it involves using a kind of vague language in

a way that they will have to fill in the blanks, mind and with their own experience.

For example, if you said, "Imagine the perfect piece of pizza, with cheese and mushrooms and some shiny anchovies on top, all topped with extra hot sauce!" Now, that would only make them hungry if they liked the same thing you liked. Most people don't like pizza with anchovies and hot sauce therefore, that sentence probably wouldn't work with many.

But how about this sentence:

"Imagine the perfect dish, right in front of you. Imagine smelling it right now, exactly the way you like it. Now, look at it. Imagine the perfect colors, the perfect shape, and the perfect size.
Imagine me giving you that right now saying, this is all for you to enjoy exactly how you want it.

That's much, much better. You have to fill in the blanks, and unless you've just eaten, you probably are starting to get a little bit hungry. And here's the best part. I don't even need to know what kind of food you like, but I've already got you imagining your favorite food. Now what if we were sitting in a park or something, and I wanted to ask you to have dinner with me. This would make it much more likely that you would join me!

The good news is that there are many, many different ways to use this technology, to use other people's ideas to get them to do just want you to want, for their own reasons. This not only means that there won't be any resistance, but it also means they'll be very glad, and want to do it again for you in the future!

How To Easily Influence Anybody According To Their Reasons

Everybody would love to be more persuasive. But most people are pretty clueless about how to persuade others. For example, if you wanted a girl to give you her number, how would you ask? You might suggest getting together later, or maybe trying to beat around the bush or something. But what if there was a way to get girls to give you their number before you even asked?

Luckily, there is a way and it involves using some of the easy to learn techniques from covert hypnosis. What is this word magic you may ask? Well, it involves speaking in a way that you're saying one thing on one level, but something else on another level.

For example, you might be talking about the people around you, the couples that you see, how they are interacting with each other. But on a deeper level, you are talking about love, and how people fall in love. And on an even deeper level, you are talking about you and her falling in love. So after only about twenty or thirty minutes of a normal-sounding conversation, she is really eager to give you her contact information, or even more.

What's more, if you are already in a relationship, you can use these powerful techniques to make her beg for you to do things to her that YOU want. Not only that, but she'll enjoy them more than ever.

Of course, it goes without saying that such a powerful technology can be abused. Many people have used these tools to get girls to fall madly in love them in a matter of minutes. But then later, when the guy is finished with her, the poor girl has her heartbroken.

Many salespeople also abuse these tools. They use them to build up massive buying temperature in their clients when they can't even afford the product! Needless to say, this is very evil and something you should never do.

But so long as you have their best interests in mind, using these techniques can significantly speed up the process of getting them very interested in whatever you want them interested in.

One word of caution though. Many people believe these are a set of language patterns to be memorized, and then used verbatim. This is definitely NOT the case. This is like learning another language. It takes time and a lot of practice. But once you learn these powerful tools, you will be able to speak to people on many different levels. The best part is they'll decide to do what you want, for their reasons. Which means they'll rarely be any resistance!

MANIPULATE THE MIND THROUGH NLP

NLP - How is Neuro-Linguistic Programming Used?

Let's start with what is NLP? NLP stands for Neuro-Linguistic Programming, which sounds pretty fancy, doesn't it? Simply NLP has been developed by studying those people who are successful in their lives. Why are they more successful than the rest of us, me and you? They have learned through training or 'Programming' their minds (the 'Neuro' part) to respond to language use (the 'Linguistic' bit). NLP is used by these successful communicators and high achieving individuals to control certain aspects of their lives to maximize their potential for success. The question you are asking yourself is if can you learn these methods as well..and the answer is yes! These people had a secret they've shared so now many people are practicing NLP in their lives and experiencing the benefits. Some people opt for training so they can become experts and help others; some people may just want a fast cure for a phobia, whilst others want to lose weight.

You may have seen Derren Brown on TV, he has become a master practitioner using many of the NLP techniques in manipulating of people and their thoughts. In fact, NLP is often referred to as a form of hypnotism, stage magic or mind control. There are many skeptics who just think it is trickery or magic, but the reality is that these techniques are real and they can be learned by anyone.

So, when considering the question of how is Neuro-Linguistic Programming used, you should also ask yourself what do you want to change in your life. NLP can be used to make changes in your personal life as for example improving your relationships with loved ones or to meet and make new friends. The techniques can be used to improve your work life, whether it's to succeed in your career, get you that dream job you have wanted, a promotion or pay rise. NLP can be used to improve your health by helping you quit smoking, lose weight and get that dream body. NLP is successfully used around the world daily to cure people of their crippling phobias. The skills and techniques you can learn will enable you to significantly reduce your stress levels, enabling you to be able to finally relax and enjoy life a little!

NLP is used in a wide range of professional areas including counseling, psychotherapy, education, health, creativity, law, management, sales, leadership, and parenting. NLP is equally useful for each and every one of us who desires a more rewarding life.

NLP - How Does Neuro-Linguistic Programming Work?

The skill and techniques utilized by practitioners of NLP enable them to break learned behaviors or habits and create new ones. If you force yourself to get up early and go for a run, before work or the kids then this requires effort. If you persevere for 30 days then it will become a habit which requires very little effort. Through NLP you can learn how to shortcut this habit-forming process. Your mind and the minds of others are there for the training. NLP allows you to see other peoples learned responses to stimuli such as how they behave in different social situations. Whilst, also giving you control to manipulate their behavior and influence their thoughts.

If you want to use NLP for motivation it teaches a technique called, 'anchoring' which essentially allows you to trigger whatever emotional response you desire e.g. determination or euphoria. Say for example you want to make regular exercise part of your normal routine without it being a huge effort; You can use the anchoring technique to induce enthusiasm whenever you think about exercising. Another excellent use of NLP techniques is to cure people of their phobias. These situations require the use of the 'swish' technique, which allows you to replace the feelings of fear and repulsion that you have learned to associate with spiders, snakes or the dark and re-learn new emotions. The 'swish' technique allows you to switch a happier thought for the learned fright response. Many of the people who are successful have learned how to 'read' people's use of language to be empathetic and increase rapport. Typically, people use descriptions with their dominant sense incorporated into their language patterns, e.g. someone whose primary sense is visual will say," I see" or "It looks good". Whilst another person whose dominant sense may be auditory could say, "Sounds good" or "That rings a bell". Then a third person (kinaesthetic) will likely say, "That doesn't feel right" or "I can't put my finger on it". To establish rapport in a conversation with these individuals an NLP practitioner will then mirror their use of language depending on the observed primary sense. One of the keys to success in life is to establish a good rapport with the people that you interact within your life, whether they are family, friends, colleagues or strangers.

The key thing to remember is that NLP works and anyone can learn how!

How Do You Protect Yourself From NLP Trickery?

I will continue in this section by looking at the world of NLP - neuro-linguistic programming. Plowing through the works of Richard Bandler, John Grinder, Milton Erikson, and Stephen Brooks opened my mind. I loved the writing style of Bandler in particular with his wordplays, his wit and his bold individuality. Yet most of all I learned that the human mind is a fragile piece of delicate machinery. It shocked me how easily the depths of the unconscious mind can be accessed by those with the right skills and how then it can be programmed and reprogrammed at will. Not without reason did Bandler and Grinder title their first book 'The Structure of Magic'.

There is much value in NLP yet I would like to see it challenged more strongly - not to prove it wrong but to raise awareness on its best practice and to tackle the unspoken risk of manipulation that it inevitably entails. In particular, I would like to propose the idea of neuro-linguistic protection as a counter skill-set to neuro-linguistic programming.

Neuro-linguistic protection would focus upon helping people develop the behaviors to protect their unconscious minds from unwanted and illicit programming. It would be like having a virus checker for the human mind or parental code to prevent access to sensitive mental sites. Whereas traditional NLP and hypnosis have focused upon putting people into a trance and so access the unconscious mind, these self-protective behaviors would focus upon waking people up and stimulating their conscious minds to stand tall and strong when necessary.

Ultimately, to protect yourself and others you must know how and when to say 'STOP!'. To point at a line in the ground and say 'No more. No further. Enough'.

Some of the behaviors required to do this skillfully and compassionately are found in the more advanced coaching models - giving challenging feedback, holding accountability, setting courageous goals, sustaining tension and raising awareness regarding the 'bigger picture' through systems thinking techniques.

In this context, advanced coaching models could be viewed as a starting point for helping others to achieve neuro-linguistic protection. It is about exploring the impact of a shared, collective reality rather than focusing upon the underlying structure of person-centered magic. It is about recognizing and respecting the limits and boundaries that are an inevitable feature of organizational life. For until we feel safe in the hands of a Bandler, an Erikson or a Brooks then would it be wise to open those inner doors and let their magic in?

WHAT IS DARK PSYCHOLOGY AND HOW TO USE IT?

A Powerful Persuasion Strategy

The reverse psychology is the paradox of psychology, according to which you try to get a positive result by a negative or vice versa suggestion.

It is a strategy where we use techniques that aim to move the person to a certain contrary action we are talking about. An example for you to understand better would be to say, "Do not keep reading this text now."

If you continued, you "fell" into one of the strategies. In Reverse Psychology, we use a counter command, the actual action we want the person to perform, as in the example above where I told you not to continue reading, my goal was exactly the opposite.

Reverse psychology is extremely effective with resistant and authoritarian people, this section today we will see some of this strategy uses.

Every human being is unique, and each person has a way of buying and/or saying "Yes" differently, a part of people will adapt better with direct orders like Buy Now, Secure Your Seat, Sign Already, etc. However, there is a group of people who will not accept orders as direct as these, in these cases the use of reverse psychology is the most appropriate.

There are several ways to use and several linguistic standards, I will cite a few:

1 - Appeal to Identity:

"Are you the kind of person that_____? then leave to (Action) important, another moment.

Example: "Are you the kind of person who does not like to make appointments? Then leave for later reading this important part "

"I bet you _____"

Example: "I bet you can not make compromises."

This pattern requires some degree of affinity with the person.

Function: The appeal to identity is good to be used when you know the person a little because this pattern will have to say the opposite of what it is so that it will do what you ask without necessarily giving you a direct order.

2 - Negative Command

"You do not need (action) now / today."

Example: "You do not need to use these patterns today."

"I'm not going to say that_____"

Example: "I will not say that using these standards will leverage your sales."

Function: This pattern uses the "No" trigger as a softener while causing the brain to make an internal representation of the action to be done, another example to clarify further is "Do not think about the color red", you certainly thought.

3 - Reinforcement of Autonomy

"I can not (Action) by you, even if (benefits). Only you can decide that. "

Example: "I can not decide to buy for you, even though this course will help you leverage your sales potential. Only you can decide that. "

Function: It strengthens the decision-making autonomy of the person, here you need to tell your clients/prospects what you can not do them do something they do not want to do even if there are many benefits in the action.

4 - Use of external authority

"Experts say____, never / hardly _____"

Example: "Experts say young entrepreneurs would hardly be able to see the benefits of this training."

Function: The point is to say that other people have said that the prospect/client will not be able to do a certain action, this causes the person to do the opposite.

The use of reverse psychology is very effective but requires care, the person can not consciously realize that you want to change their behaviors, so in order to have an effective result, you need to be nothing obvious and use them subtly.

I bet you will not use these techniques in your scripts.

Some Reverse Psychology Considerations

Reverse psychology is a complicated subject both in real life and in psychological studies. Researchers have found that it is difficult to determine exactly when reversing psychology works and when it does not. However, we can point out some factors that may increase psychological reactance:

- The more attractive and important the thing being restricted, the greater the psychological effect.

- The greatest psychological retardant is a deprivation of liberty.
- Threats involving some form of decision-making produce a greater level of retardation, as it does not make much sense, leaves people even more rebellious.

In real life, reverse psychology works best when used sparingly and subtly, applying mostly to people who are resistant to requests.

Rapport: The Secret Art of the Masters of Persuasion

"Rapport is the ability to get into someone's world, make you feel that you understand it and that you have a strong bond in common. It is the ability to go all the way from your world map to your world map. It is the essence of successful communication. " -Anthony Robbins

Rapport: What is it?

Rapport is a word of French origin and has no translation into Portuguese, however, within NLP create Rapport can be understood as the establishment of trust, harmony, and cooperation in a relationship.

Trust lowers interpersonal tension and makes the future (or current) client more comfortable. It opens up more freely and reveals information about your needs, desires, goals, dreams and personal fears. Without trust is extremely difficult and in some cases even impossible to sell something, even if the product or service is the best in the world.

"People love to buy, but they hate it when you try to sell them something!"

When you create an atmosphere of trust and harmony with a person, the transition from the relationship to the sales dialogue is simple and extremely effective. Behavioral reactions are much more effective.

When you try to sell something without creating a relationship the brain processes all the information differently, and before you even try to make any closing the sale will already be lost, because the last meta-message is that you just want to sell and nothing else. You may even succeed, but it will only be a short-term result.

Now, when you establish rapport, in addition to the ease you will have to sell, you will build a relationship that will enable long-term sales. Not to mention the objections that will be almost nil.

Benefits of the technique

Rapport is a fantastic NLP technique and with it, you will get numerous benefits, I will mention a few below:

- It is one of the fastest and most efficient ways to generate "trust" in a dialogue.

- We rely on people who are similar to us, so it is easier to suggest/persuade their interlocutor, whether to sell a product or to change or even change a belief - I do not speak in the religious sense but in an absolute truth about something that the person believes.

- When we understand someone it is easier to lead them by the right path.

- Increase your interpersonal relationships.

- Enhance a relationship.

- Establish trust instantly.

Universal Elements of Rapport

- Smile - is the universal key of Rapport.
- Optimism - conveys confidence and a sense of power.
- Treat your other by name - the most beautiful sound anyone can hear is that of your pronounced name.
- Patience - know how to listen, because when someone speaks it is because they want to be listened to.

How to Create Rapport?

To get Rapport you can mirror any part of your partner's behavior by adjusting your verbal and non-verbal behavior to move along with it. This is the same as giving a command to the person's unconscious mind, telling them to trust you because it is similar to him.

This technique reaches an unconscious level, therefore it has to be done with MESSAGE, ELEGANCE, AND SUBTELTY, otherwise, it will irritate your interlocutor, because it will seem like a child wanting to imply with his colleague imitating all his gestures.

Behavior that can be mirrored:

- **Body Movements:** Choose any movement of the body that is constant and mirror. E.g.: If the person is gesturing too much with the arms, the moment you return to speak repeat the same movements that your interlocutor did when expressing himself.
- **Vocal qualities:** equalize tone, volume, rhythm, velocity, and so on.
- Words: use the words that she uses and/or emphasize, also use your preferred terms, even if they are wrong, but it is what matters to your interlocutor.

- **Breathing:** Equalize your breathing at the same pace as the other person's breathing. (This is the strongest, and you can do it halfway.) To find out which channel is preferential - Auditory, visual or kinesthetic - to know what kind of breathing - thoracic, abdominal or intermediate.
- **Facial expressions:** Raise eyebrows, squeeze lips, wrinkle nose, and nod while the person talks.

These are some of the possible mirrorings. I emphasize that always do the mirroring SUBTLE way so that the technique becomes effective. Another important thing is that the fundamental basis of the Rapport is the accompaniment, that is, first accompany and then drive, it is like a dance, first, you accompany your pair in the rhythm of the music and soon after that, it will accompany you. At a high level of Rapport, it is possible that the person begins to mirror you, at the moment the person accepts the suggestion, the negotiation, the seduction and more.

How to create rapport on the internet?

To create rapport on the internet you must mirror the communication of the person you are talking to. Below I will list 4 tips for you to start using today:

1. When writing to someone, or even chatting, use the person's name whenever possible. Doing so will generate trust and empathy, for by reading the person you will be unconsciously making associations, usually positive, to you.

2. Find the way to write and mirror a few words. If the person writes using slang, consider using some in the conversation. If she abbreviated words, also consider abbreviating some.

3. Ask questions to discover common interests. Anything you and your partner share the same idea will increase the level of empathy.

4. Use emotions in your communication. If you are talking about a sad or happy subject, use the emotions that represent this emotional state, it also increases the level of empathy between you.

All rapport techniques serve to create a climate of harmony and trust, the message you are sending directly to the person's unconscious is that you are alike. We trust who is like us and by showing this to a person, whether online or face-to-face you will increase your chances of success 100%.

MIND CONTROL TECHNIqUES

How psychopaths use it?

The basic techniques of mind control are widely used by sects to capture, indoctrinate and maintain members, and most leaders are psychopaths. Here we will take a look at what Robert Hare, an expert in psychopathy, says about the techniques used by psychopaths to start a relationship with someone in order to dominate and control them.

These ideas about basic mind control techniques can easily be applied to one-to-one relationships and groups.

Understanding People

First of all, psychopaths can be very effective in scanning people. Probably because they work very hard on it! Its main motivation is to control and dominate people and have developed an effective strategy to achieve it.

They can evaluate people very quickly, assessing their strengths and also their weaknesses. And the more information you have about someone, the more influence they will have in terms of manipulating that person.

Who is vulnerable?

So, who do these basic mind control techniques work with? Unfortunately, the answer is ... with everyone! Learn about specific vulnerabilities here.

Hare explains that there are three aspects of personality that we need to consider.

We have our intimate or private personality which is what we feel inside. Including our thoughts, attitudes, preferences, values, emotions, hopes, ambitions and our positive traits. Also, the negative traits that we can try to hide, and sometimes we want to improve, and other times we simply try to forget or ignore them.

The public self, or person, is the way we want others to think about us. It is what you reveal about yourself to others, hoping that they will see the best of you. We try to maximize our good things and minimize the bad ones.

The third aspect is reputation, how others see us in reality. Despite our best efforts, people form their own impressions based on their opinions, beliefs, and values. All these filters and distortions of information cause more changes in how people see us.

An important point is that People form first impressions very quickly, often seconds later to meet someone. As time passes, they look for information to confirm their initial impressions and tend to ignore information that contradicts their first impressions. These are natural biases in the decision making of the human being.

So, if we like someone from the beginning, we will like them more and more. Robert Cialdini points to this as one of the six weapons of influence. It is important because if we like someone, they are more likely to be influenced by this person.

Hare also talks about consistency, another of Cialdini's weapons of influence. When a person's words and actions seem to be consistent, we rely on them.

We can have big problems if our first impressions are wrong!

The man who agrees with everything you say or is a fool or is preparing to skin you.

- Kin Hubbard

So, how does this work?

When a psychopath knows someone new, he evaluates it according to his usefulness or the value he has for him. Evaluate your personality Robert Hare says that the face, the words, and your body language are an autobiography written in capital letters!

Based on your personality, the psychopath begins to project a character that allows him to create a close and intimate relationship with you. This bond becomes the basis for further manipulation and for mind control.

The psychopath evaluates your weaknesses and strengths, looking for your insecurities, needs and the things you value. Then, your actions and your words send four important messages to you:

1. I like who you are
2. I am like you
3. Your secrets are safe with me
4. I am the perfect friend, partner, lover, partner, boyfriend ... for you!

These basic mind control techniques may not occur in a strict sequence, there are many that will overlap, or jump from one to another. However, they work to influence our decision making. Let's examine this in the next section.

The Key To Mind Control

What is this?

The key to mind control that distinguishes mind control from brainwashing is in the way the manipulator is perceived by the "victim." In brainwashing, the manipulator is a clear enemy.

Physical strength is often used. The person may be in a position where his life depends on accepting the wishes of the manipulator.

The key to mind control is that the victim believes that the manipulator is a friend, or a teacher, or someone who has his heart's best wishes.

It means that the manipulated person is willing to participate, believes that she is being helped and is taking care of her. He believes he is making his own decisions. This makes it more dangerous than pointing someone with a gun to the head!

We have explained how a psychopath very quickly creates an intimate bond after having assessed the personality of the victim and creating a character that is attractive to that personality.

The psychopath gives 4 messages:

1. I like who you are
2. I am like you
3. Your secrets are safe with me
4. I am the perfect friend, partner, lover, boyfriend ... for you!

Let's take a closer look at the key to mind control, how and why these messages deceive the victim into believing that the psychopath is a friend.

I LIKE WHO YOU ARE

We all want to be loved. We want them to realize about us and be accepted. We all like compliments. Having someone who is attentive to us (when most people are concerned with themselves) is flattering in itself.

Accepting and reinforcing someone's personality is an incredibly powerful method to get someone to like them. And psychopaths will do it in a very captivating, charming, and with manners! They are experts in knowing the key to mind control.

I am LIKE YOU

Based on what the psychopath knows about you, thanks to what you say, but more importantly because of the assessment he has made about you, the psychopath begins to share details about his own life. It seems as if he is lowering his guard. However, they are often simply lying. The things you share are precisely about issues that are important to you. This begins to strengthen the bond.

YOUR SECRETS ARE SAFE WITH ME

Because they share "intimate details" with you, it's easy to let your guard down and start talking about yourself. After all, you feel in the company of someone who really understands you, who understands you on a deeper level than most people. You trust that person is different and you get absorbed by this mental control trick.

The psychopath is filling another of our basic psychological, security, physical and emotional needs.

I AM THE PERFECT FRIEND, COMPANION, LOVER, BOYFRIEND ... FOR YOU!

So you think that you have really found someone who understands you and accepts you for who you are, "with all your faults". The more information you give to the psychopath, the character he projects the more seems to fit for you.

You build a strong reputation for it in your mind, perhaps with similar weaknesses, perhaps with skills, you would like to have. The relationship is different and special in many ways.

The psychopath has done his job to take you to this point, and now your destiny is linked to this psychopathic link.

As I mentioned earlier, this can happen in a one-to-one relationship, or in groups.

Is not this normal?

So, why are these considered as basic mind control techniques? Do not these things happen between husband and wife, for example? Of course yes.

The difference is that the psychopathic relationship is not real. The character of the psychopath has been built. As far as the psychopath is concerned, there is no such relationship. He has simply made it manipulate you. He has said everything that is necessary to convince you about something, while he is organizing something else.

A psychopath said "(In the context of a relationship ...) if you do not know who is directing, you are the one being led by the nose. "

It means that there was no informed choice on your part. The psychopath deliberately chooses you based on what you can get for your benefit. You have no idea what is really happening.

It Will Not Last

These relationships are not going to last, in two ways. As soon as you are hooked, the psychopath changes and does only the minimum to maintain the relationship. All the "supposed" initial care, attention and love can disappear. For example, if a psychopathic woman builds a relationship with a man and marries him, her behavior toward him will change drastically, toward manipulation and abuse.

The second way it will not last is when the psychopath does not find more use in that person and discards it. Literally. The person is disconcerted, does not understand what has happened, and even wishes the psychopath returns!

Everything is about power!

These relationships have an imbalance of power, obviously, the power resides in the psychopath. This is the goal of this key to mind control - winning and maintaining power and control over others.

(The imbalance of power means that there is no informed consent in sexual relationships where one of the parties is under mental control, legally known as sexual assault or sexual abuse.)

Most people like to think that there is something good in each one of us. Do you remember how we form our first impressions based on our beliefs and values? Most people expect others to be good, respectful and honest in their relationships, and that is what they look for in others.

One of the reasons why psychopaths are so successful is that people do not believe that such evil exists. Evil is a common word in the description of psychopaths, it is not simply a matter of taking advantage over other people, there are social predators hunting victims. Like reptiles, they have no conscience!

They are quite happy to use this key of mind control to abuse people psychologically, emotionally, sexually, physically, work and financially, all without guilt or remorse, and the slightest regard for their victims!

Watch out!

If you feel that your relationship is almost perfect and that it has happened very quickly, use this as a signal that you need to stop and re-evaluate what is happening. This is an opportunity to stop mind control before you are negatively affected.

Mental Control Tactics And Pseudo Personalities Purpose

What are the mind control tactics designed for? Obviously to control the mind of people, control their thoughts, and in this way control their emotions and their behaviors.

In George Orwell's 1984 book, a member of the totalitarian regime says: "Thought is the only thing that matters, we do not just destroy our enemies, we change them, it is intolerable for us that a wrong thinking exist anywhere in the world, however, it can be secret and less powerful, even at the moment of death we can not allow ourselves any deviation. "

More Specifically...

The best description for the result of mind control tactics is Edgar Schein's three-step process, the process of unfreezing, changing and refreezing the identity or personality. He wrote about this in his book on coercive persuasion after studying brainwashing programs in China in the 1950s.

- Defrosting is literally breaking the person, making him doubt himself and his reality.
- Change is the process of indoctrination, installation of new beliefs, values, ideas, etc., and
- Re-freezing is the strengthening and solidification of the new identity, the pseudo-identity, or sometimes called pseudo-personality.

We think of the pseudo-personality as a personality that represses and dominates the pre-sect personality (before the sect). It is not and should not be confused with multiple personalities. To a large extent, it is a clone of the leader of the sect, with the same ideas, beliefs, values, and behaviors.

Often these are very different from what the person had before!

Janja Lalich describes it this way:

The central "I" of a person develops throughout life - encompasses all the ways in which the person approaches, reacts, and copes with emotions, relationships, and events. Each person develops psychological defense mechanisms that he uses to perceive, interpret and face reality. A systematic attack on the part of the central ego of the person separates him from the internal balance and the perception of reality.

For some, Margaret Singer realizes that the *"easiest way to rebuild her central self and get a new balance is to"* identify with the aggressor *"and accept the ideology of the authority figure that has reduced the person to a In fact, the new ideology (psychological theory, the spiritual system, etc.) functions as a defense mechanism ... and protects the individual from having to continue to directly inspect the emotions of the past that are so overwhelming."*

Recognizing this attack on a person's psychological stability and defense mechanisms is fundamental to understanding why some sects achieve such rapid and dramatic ideological acceptance, and why many sects can generate psychological difficulties and other adjustment problems in members. .

The goal of a thought reform program is to change a human being from its center so that it will believe in a certain ideology, doctrine, or leader - and adapt and behave accordingly. Once the feat has been established, the follow-up or obedience of the followers or the intimate partner (in the case of abusive relationships) is usually guaranteed.

These ideas that are the result of mind control tactics can lead members to do such radical things as break relationships with family and friends, leave their jobs, donate their savings or income to the group, and even commit murder or suicide. The degree of change usually depends on how long a person has been in the group, the number and intensity of the techniques and tools used, the activities of the members in the sect, how much hypnosis has been used, among other things.

Thus, for example, many destructive sects today have members who live in their own homes and continue with their jobs. However, their beliefs may have changed considerably and with that their attitudes and behaviors. Mind control tactics work "at a distance," so to speak.

Features

One of the common characteristics is an attitude of superiority, members believe they are better or know more than those around them. This makes sense when you consider that you are copying a psychopath!

However, it is another contradiction of the sects, because for the members their reality, in fact, has been reduced, and their decision making takes place within this bounded, limited reality. His ability to think critically has been severely reduced by mind control tactics.

They will not tolerate any criticism towards the group or the leader and may sound like a tape recording giving information about the group or defending the leader or his own acts.

Usually and typically the members of a group will insist that they are happy, even saying that they have never been happier! In general, they will refuse any kind of help, especially from psychologists or psychiatrists because the groups have indoctrinated them against these people.

In the worst case, due to mental control tactics, their memory and comprehension are reduced, the vocabulary is minimized, they lose their sense of humor and are unable to make decisions to solve problems. Their behavior becomes very childish and they blindly do whatever the leader tells them.

The Inner World

Internally, there is often a great mental conflict for members of the sect. First of all, they feel responsible for every wrong thing in their lives. They blame themselves for anything that goes wrong, or they feel bad, or if they have done something they should not have done, etc. They are also, in general, hyper-alert in terms of trying to please the group and the leader.

In addition to this, Steve Hassan says that the members of a sect are at war with themselves. The pseudo-personality may be doing things that the real personality would never do. Anything from lies to criticize other members to leaders, or sexual promiscuity, to murder. Or the person witnesses other things that happen in the group with which they disagree, but the pseudo-personality provides reasons, excuses, and justifications for why it is okay.

What happens next ...?

Even after a person leaves a group, and is free of mind control tactics, the personality persists. Remember that the group member believes that he (alone) has made his own decisions about the ideas and beliefs he has adopted, so they tend to last a long time. They do not realize that they have a pseudo-personality. Cults do not realize exactly this fact when they are picking up people!

In some cases, members have symptoms so severe because of this, that they can be diagnosed as schizophrenic, psychotic, or with multiple personality disorders, personality disorder, etc. The symptoms may look a lot like post-traumatic stress disorder.

quite often former members of sects have difficulty keeping their jobs out of the group, or maintaining relationships or even being in social groups. These difficulties can last for years and may never be resolved.

Not until they realize they have been in a sect and have been subjected to mind control tactics can they begin to undo the pseudo-personality, and often, this requires the help of professionals.

Let's examine some of the most common mind control tactics used in the next stages of thawing, shifting and freezing ...

Control Techniques And Their Purposes

In the internal sectarian dynamics, a series of secret practices are carried out that have as a common denominator the control of their followers. Most people think of mind control when talking about control techniques. But the truth is that control extends beyond the mind and reaches the very structure of the subject's personality.

The control techniques are exercised through a network of procedures, strategies, resources, and influences that destroys the original identity of the subject (beliefs, feelings, emotions, dignity, behavior, thought, etc.) and replaces it with another whose characteristic Most outstanding is the docility before the orders, the subjection and the psychological dependence. The success of the capture of victims in dangerous sects depends on the annulment of the original person to transform it into an insecure, restless and fearful subject; easy to manipulate, dominate, intimidate and control. For this they use techniques of coercive persuasion or techniques of mind control and brainwashing; caused by the Induced suggestion or autosuggestion. They seek to stop thinking or logical reasoning.

The set of procedures and resources used to achieve these ends is known by different names: coercive persuasion, persuasion techniques, techniques of mind control, brainwashing, mental manipulation, induced suggestion, self - suggestion (self - hypnosis), techniques to stop thinking, etc. No matter the name, whatever the name used, all are reduced to the same. They bring the same consequences. They pursue the same purposes. They share many of the characteristics. They are methods whose ultimate goal is to cause the destruction of critical judgment, the will and the freedom of decision of the people. They seek to subdue and manipulate their victims through deception and psychological dependence. They are practiced with systematic regularity and mathematical precision. They are exercised with increasing force over their victims; causing even serious psychological disorders.

All the techniques are directed to control:

- the victim's behavior
- the information that the victim receives, processes and uses
- the ideas that make up the victim's everyday thoughts
- the intimate feelings and emotions of the victim
- the personal, professional, family and social environment of the victim

That is why they end up destroying the original personality of the subject subjects, who transform their way of acting, feeling, thinking and perceiving reality. Hence, the sects that use them are evaluated as destructive groups. The ability to reason, to make decisions, to differentiate reality from imagined, truth and falsehood, to recognize the reasonableness of the irrational, etc. they are systematically destroyed. The subjects become authentic human dolls willing to execute any order of their leaders without subjecting it to prior evaluation. Sometimes, even, the victims go to the extreme of sacrificing themselves to death because of the doctrines defended by the leader and the group.

The dangerousness of these techniques is hidden in the secrecy and isolation that often characterize these dangerous groups. It is within the secrecy and loyalty demanded of the sectarian adepts that the techniques of control and mental domination are most successful. The lack of knowledge that ordinary people have about these techniques, together with the secrecy that hides them from public scrutiny, increases the likelihood that they will succeed in the victims. Nobody usually escapes their effects if they ignore how they work. And everyone is susceptible to fall into the networks of these strategies. That is why no one should underestimate the effectiveness of the control techniques used by sects.

It is important to expose these methods to the public. The more knowledge and information we have about them, the greater will be the opportunities to recognize the danger behind these resources. The information about sects and their internal dynamics is the best defense against them.

In the following descriptive list, we try to expose the most frequent techniques. We warn that they are not the only ones. Most of these techniques are not offered in their chemically pure state. In general, they are refined, improved, mixed, individualized and individualized so that they serve better and more efficiently, according to the moment and the victim. In addition, sects often recycle and reinvent the techniques of deception and destruction continuously.

This list that we present below is not intended to be final. It does not even pretend to be exhaustive. We only present it as an example of the dynamics that are carried out in secret within the sects. I invite you to reflect on other ways of control. Surely there are.

A. *Mortifications*

Is the set of actions whose purpose is to afflict the subjects and cause them the greatest possible amount of distress and discomfort (both physically, as psychological, emotional, spiritual, moral, etc.). They are presented in the form of suitable opportunities for the victim to tame their passions, punishing, for example, their body or restraining their will, because it is assumed that the bodily needs, such as rest or food, seriously hinder and damage the commitment of the adept with the group. In addition, wanting to satisfy these needs is a manifestation of the ego. Therefore, the adept must deny himself, embrace the ideas of the group and defend them with his life, if necessary.

The repertoire of sacrifices invented by dangerous sects is long, extensive and varied. Here we only present some:

- **Penance** - Imposition of punishments destined to purify a fault or bad action. It is likely that the lack or bad action is only an invention or use of the leader to create the perfect scenario for punishment. In general, the penance does not keep harmony with the supposed fault committed. The lack is just an excuse to punish the adept. Penance can be public or private; personal or group. The period of time varies, depending on the bad action that you want to purify.

- **Humiliations** - They are generally public. They indoctrinate them to accept humiliation voluntarily, making them believe that accepting it is an act of true humility and in some sects are considered a healthy and timely exercise to practice the " Denial of the Self", therefore, it is just and deserved. They have the double intention of aggravating the victim and exalting the leader. The humiliated subject is considered a bad person who should not be respected; he is worthy of humiliation; is ignored and, sometimes, even disowned by the group. The victim becomes a counter-model: an example that should never be imitated. The real message hidden in the humiliations is "if you do not want to be in your place, you must obey".

- **Punishments** - Combination of humiliations and penances performed before an audience that watches helplessly, unable to say anything without the ability to issue its judgment. The person punished is trampled on his dignity as a human person; his affections and feelings are the objects of mockery and ridicule. or Sacrifices. They can be taxes (daily prayers, fasts, painful exercises, etc.)

- **Suggested Sacrifices** - (those who perform them are considered superior to the rest of the group). In many cases instruments have used that help to make the corporal sacrifices more effective: whips with spines, sackcloths, etc. As the latter are only suggested, it is considered that the subject agrees to perform them on his person by his own will. Nothing is further from this perception. Group pressure, the anxiety of recognition, the desire to be accepted by the group and the pressure of the leader, act on the victim as reasons that justify the sacrifices.

Sleep deprivation or rest. The physical and psychological rest that is achieved through normal and continuous sleep for a reasonable time is a basic need of every human being. Therefore, depriving or preventing their satisfaction in a systematic and continuous manner is a practice that threatens the personal health of the subjects. Lack of sufficient amount of sleep can occur for psychological or somatic reasons (sleep disorders), by personal decision or by deliberate induction.

It should be noted that several studies have shown that selective sleep deprivation can produce, after a few days, even temporary psychosis. This last way of sleep deprivation is frequently used by destructive and dangerous sects.

Through the induction of sleep deprivation, these groups pursue a gradual physical, psychological and moral weakening that facilitates the manipulation and control of people.

Some of the techniques and procedures through which it is possible to induce loss of rest are:

- **Irregular meeting times** - The more irregular and untimely the meeting hours, the greater the opportunity to induce the effects of fatigue and anxiety that is desired. The decision making in these meetings at the wrong time does not find great obstacles or oppositions among the adepts, because what is desired is to finish as soon as possible to go to rest.

- **Interruption in normal sleep schedules** - Calling in the wee hours of the morning to satisfy a desire of the leader, respond to a specific requirement or need or, simply to answer a question or doubt, become sufficient reasons to wake up the followers. Sometimes they are forced to get up early after a meeting that has ended late at dawn, to continue the work of the meeting.

- **Appropriation of personal time** - Adepts who have reached higher levels in the hierarchy of command, do not have personal time to devote to their family, their person or intimate and professional matters. The time of each one must be "donated" to the sect. Whereupon, the right to sleep and rest is normally considered a selfish manifestation.

- **Extreme limitation of rest time** - Like the sect and, in its name, the leader, is the owner of the time of the most loyal and faithful followers, they must learn to limit their resting time to the maximum. The adept is made to believe that the less he sleeps, the more time he can give the group and the greater sanctity, respect and elevation he will have within the sectarian hierarchy.

- **Overloaded schedule of tasks to be done in the shortest possible time** - The adept has to perform specific tasks, numerous and varied with a timetable schedule and deadlines. The affairs of the sect are always urgent and more important than their own. In this way, the adept is always busy, he does not have time to "think" of himself and his needs and he becomes an extremely manageable being. Sleeping while having pending tasks to perform is impossible and is considered a lack of responsibility, dignity, and respect towards the group.

It is easy to infer that a subject with this circumstantial situation is easily controlled and manipulated.

According to studies conducted around the lack of sleep and rest, the consequences can be varied and complex. The theory that sees in the dream a "somatic" process, supported by Freud and that still prevails as the most accepted today, was exposed by W. Robert in 1886. The theory suggests that the dream has the faculty to help organize impressions or ideas, that remain unfinished in our thought and have only touched it fugitively, in a logical and coherent way. This author has to his theory on two proven facts: how often the most secondary day impressions are included in our dreams and how rarely we dream of what most interested us in our waking life.

This concludes the assumption that a man who is stripped of the faculty of dreaming, will soon contract a disturbance or mental disorder, because in his brain will accumulate a mass of unfinished thoughts, not finished thinking and insignificant impressions, under whose weight would be drowned that which should be incorporated into memory. In this way, patterns of inconsistency in his behavior, insecurity, and confusion develop, which could increase a sense of dependence on the criterion of a source of trust, due to the increase in his distrust of his own decisions, analysis, and judgment. It also lends itself to the possibility that due to all the missing pieces to logically compose the puzzle of your thoughts.

Multiple studies point to the effects of sleep deprivation on memory and learning functions. The REM sleep deprivation makes it difficult to remember the learning of wakefulness, makes it difficult to acquire learning the next day, but does not alter the consolidation of simple learning. Cognitive performance decreases during long periods of sleep deprivation. In several sleep experiments, it has been found that selective deprivation can produce, after a few days:

- ❖ difficulty in fixing the attention, inability to follow a straight line of thought, decreased concentration and rational capacity, a disjunction of associations
- ❖ spatial and temporal disorientation
- ❖ memory deficits
- ❖ daytime drowsiness with micro - dreams, and awakenings
- ❖ affective and behavioral alterations: fear, stress, clinical depression, aggressiveness, causing depressive or manic features, anxiety, etc.
- ❖ disorders, loss of the sense of reality and altered states of consciousness, depersonalization, psychosis, illusions, visual and auditory hallucinations
- ❖ loosening of its usual defense mechanisms
- ❖ In younger patients suffering from this symptom, school failures and behavior disorders have been described

Physiological and neurological effects can be manifested, as well as negative psychological and moral ones. Although these effects are reversible after prolonged periods of rest, they are still extremely dangerous because of the immediate consequences they may entail. E l greater danger of excessive daytime sleepiness is the high risk of accidents and labor. Numerous studies have confirmed this phenomenon. Imagine, for example, an adept with a lack of sleep who has to drive a car to attend a meeting at dawn. The weight of fatigue can be fatal.

B. Intimidation

It is the technique in which fear, terror and panic are used to obtain from the other what is ordered. Bullying can manifest itself in the form of:

- physical, psychological or moral threats
- body language as they are murky looks, rude gestures • expletives or verbal abuse
- warnings or suggestions of abuse
- emotional harassment, blackmail

What is said or implied in the threats is rarely fulfilled in reality. However, its effect and efficiency are based on adept's belief that the threat will be fulfilled. That is why it is enough to warn him, verbally or with gestures, what awaits him if he does not obey. Thus, for example, in a dangerous Marian-type sect the adept is constantly reminded that if he does not keep his promise of loyalty and fidelity, he will win eternal damnation.

C. Isolation and Alienation

Separating the followers of their family, professional and social environment causes helplessness and loneliness. The isolation manifests itself in difficulty to communicate with other subjects that are not of the sect. In this process, the ability to receive non-recycled information, different from that provided inside the sect, is lost. Without external references, different from those provided in the interior of the sect, the adept is isolated from information that can give another insight into what is happening. A subject in these conditions is easy to control.

How To Manipulate People: 10 Mental Manipulation Techniques

Today we are going to talk about how to manipulate people? How to manipulate a man? How to manipulate a woman? In short, how to manipulate a person and how to influence someone. In this section, I will show you everything you need to know about this.

Many of you want to learn how to manipulate and ask

for mental manipulation techniques. However, know that it is quite difficult for me to answer you as there are many taboos on this issue (because people have the understandable fear of being manipulated, they do not want me to teach manipulation). Nevertheless, we are going to talk here about the art of manipulation, the art of manipulation.

Indeed, I do not think that the handling of people should remain a taboo subject. You have to be aware of several things. First of all, I'm not going to explain here how to control people: there is no such thing as pure mind control. Then we are manipulated daily on TV, by advertising, by politicians, etc. So, knowing how to manipulate people will allow you to understand how to no longer be. Finally, each technique of mental manipulation, each mentalist technique, each technique of mentalism, each technique of influence will help you to optimize your chances of obtaining what you want in life. Never force people, just by putting the odds on your side.

The 10 effective techniques to manipulate people

How to handle people # 1: Get a service

When offered something, the human being feels indebted and usually tries, as quickly as possible, to give a service in return to feel relieved, and thus relieve himself of this sense of obligation he feels. This is why many brands give free samples of their products!

Consciously or not, in the human mind, the fact of contracting a debt generates the fact of having to settle it. It is a rule that is the cement of social bond, even in primitive human societies. However, the violation of the rule of reciprocity is badly perceived, which makes its success. That's why having you do a service weaves a bond of trust with the person and makes it easier to manipulate later. Nevertheless, beware, there are people that make it uncomfortable, even put angry, to owe something to someone.

Another aspect of the rule of reciprocity: there is another principle, that of reciprocal concession. When an individual makes a request that is initially refused, and that he reformulates his request, he makes a concession and therefore tends to respond with a reciprocal concession.

To manipulate someone, ask something rather than give something. For example, ask for a small service rather than return one. Or, ask for something you do not really want and then rephrase your request by pretending to make a concession.

How to handle people #2: Use the person's first name

It is very important for the human brain to be able to name actions, things, and people. A name on a face and presto, it's no longer the unknown. It is no longer "the mass". A name, just like a word, makes things concrete.

In addition, the first name is often the first word known and retained by the baby. This creates a special connection between the baby's first name and himself. A kind of anchor. So, people who use the first name to address someone (even if they hardly know him) seem immediately more friendly and familiar. Two criteria that promote manipulation.

Have you ever heard someone say your name without addressing you? Yet you have surely returned or at least felt concerned at that moment. It was stronger than you! This is proof that there is a strong emotional connection between your first name and yourself. As a result, the next time an unknown person asks for your name and uses it to formulate his requests, you will know that he is trying to manipulate you!

How to handle people # 3: You are free to choose

The human being likes to feel free of his choices. Paradoxically, that he is explicitly told "that he is free", leads him to accept a request more easily, because he is convinced that this choice is his. When people feel that the idea comes from them, it's very easy to get them to do what we want.

What is practical with this technique of manipulation is that it can easily be combined with another thus strengthening the impact of both!

How to handle people # 4: Even nothing would help me

The fact is that people are afraid to refuse small contributions, perhaps for fear of being stingy.

Anyway, asking for money or service and saying "even a little better than nothing" or "even a little help me" optimizes the chances of actually receiving help.

Except that the thing is that the principle of coherence can quickly take over. For example, if you ask for money and say "even 10 cents is better than nothing", the person is likely to take out his wallet. Then, once she has it in her hand, she may be tempted to give more, like $ 1. Except that if you asked him $ 1 directly, you probably would not get anything.

How to manipulate people #5: Flattery

Contrary to popular belief, flattery is a manipulative technique that works. However, you have to think a little about what you are saying.

If you respect this condition, then even if the person knows that you are flattering, she will be sensitive to it. However, beware, this technique does not work if the person you are trying to handle does not think you are sincere to a minimum.

Flattery is a manipulative technique that belongs to the family of live demonstrations. A pseudo-spirit of family and belonging is created by embracing, affective demonstrations, tenderness, and flattery. And it is very effective because the individual feels immediately taken in a new family, welcoming, etc.

How to handle people #6: Give a reason

Our brain is wired to accept a request more when it is accompanied by a reason.

Even if it's a weird reason "Can I go before you in the queue because I have to go make photocopies afterward?"

Know that to manipulate people, you can choose to give a justification. Even if your argument is foolish, the person will be tempted to say yes. More, in any case, than if you do not bother to argue.

I know it sounds like a bluff, but it really works.

How to handle people # 7: Foot in the door

The foot in the door is a very well known handling technique.

In fact, asking a little favor to someone is a good way to put in place a "dynamic" persuasion. Then you present him with your "real" request.

This technique is in the logical follow-up of that which consisted of being rendered a small service. Except that here, instead of playing on reciprocity, we play on commitment and consistency.

The person answered yes to your first request or did you a small service, you can ask something more important. The person is more likely to say yes because she wants to justify the fact that she has already helped you and because you have built a pseudo trust.

How to handle people # 8: The door to the nose

The trick is based on the power of human guilt. It's the opposite of the foot in the door. Here, you are going to ask for something huge or ridiculous in order to get a no.

When the answer NO finally arrives, you present a second query that is more reasonable (but which is true from the start of course).

By the way, if by some miracle the person accesses your first "huge" query, so much the better! But most often, she will accept the second.

How to handle people # 9: Fear and then relief

When you report a clear and urgent danger to the person, it's more than just getting your attention.

But to use this technique effectively, you have to create this state of emergency through fear. Then behind, you must immediately offer relief to this fear.

Fear and relief and the creation of a sense of urgency are two diabolically effective manipulative techniques.

However, it goes without saying that this technique is very moderately ethical; it is besides that that many politicians have passed reforms that the people would never have accepted otherwise!

How to handle people # 10: The red scarf

The red scarf technique consists of pretending to refuse something reluctantly in order to have a better chance of getting a reward (what we actually wanted from the beginning).

For example, to better understand a divorce where we insist on having the dog and then at the last moment we would pretend to give it reluctantly in compensation for something else like a trinket (that we wanted to actually from the beginning). The other party will leave us thinking they have won.

THE BEST TECHNIqUES TO SPEED READING AND ANALYSE ANYONE

An Introduction to Speed Reading

Ever heard of speed reading and wondered what it was? We have all been taught to read and learn since we were kids. How did we all begin the journey? We read out aloud our favorite stories, read out aloud our textbooks so that the listener, be it a parent or a teacher could correct our pronunciations. Over the years, as we had better wisdom, we have been reading to ourselves with that tiny inner voice acting as a medium to convert the text into audio.

Speed reading is not about skimming or scanning information while you read, but its reading through and between words, culling out the information that you need. It is just a myth that speed readers can not really assimilate the information that they read. Speed readers look for the information that they need while reading and that helps them read faster.

When we read, we are not reading word by word but actually, read words by blocks. A speed reader picks the words that are required to make sense of the whole sentence and moves on unlike a slow reader who tries to understand the meaning of all words to make sense of the sentence. Also, a speed reader seldom needs to go back to words that he has already passed to comprehend the sentence. This creates a flow of reading and helps the reader to read faster.

Having read about speed reading, the reader may be wondering how to differentiate one from a normal reader. By accepted standards, a normal reader reads at a pace of 250 words a minute while a speed reader would read anywhere between 1000 to 14000 words a minute. Now if you could master reading at 14000 words a minute without compromising on comprehension, you could finish off a normal eBook in less than a minute!

Speed reading is not about the tradeoff between faster reading and better comprehension, but in the long run, as you master this tool you will be able to hold more information in your short term memory. There are various ways to get started to master this technique. The best way is to self-start, probably with the emails that you receive. You could also take help from speed reading software. The software would guide you through the initial stages when you feel you cannot be on your own feet.

As in mastering any technique, there is no shortcut to becoming a good speed reader. The best and the time tested way is to practice the technique once you are introduced to it. It is not a miracle that will happen overnight to many of us, but we can be good speed readers with diligence and hard work.

In a nutshell, speed reading is a collation of techniques which helps you read faster yet comprehend the information available. It can be fun learning and sustaining speed reading especially when you have millions of word materials, be it books or magazines or newspapers, to be read in just one lifetime!

7 quick Reading Techniques And How To Improve Your Understanding

Are you looking to develop the speed of reading? What quick reading techniques do you know? What are the benefits of learning to read faster?

On the one hand, take advantage of time in a productive way, learn something new, whether it is a hobby, places to meet, new options to continue studying, etc.

On the other hand, the world of business, where you will find abundant information to consume, manuals, publications on policies, rules, procedures, competitors and more.

In the business environment, knowing how to read faster, gives you the opportunity to optimize your daily schedule, in time and effort to get up to date in situations that affect or represent opportunities for the company.

Below I share 7 quick reading techniques,

emphasizing having a balance between reading quickly and understanding what is consumed.

Before the rapid reading techniques develop the habit to read

As a previous step to carry out a methodology to improve the speed of reading, it is necessary to acquire the habit to read.

For more techniques you practice, the advantages with fast reading will be minimal if you read very little, you are not attracted to books, magazines, blogs.

Why learn to read faster, if you feel that it is not adding value?

It is important to be convinced of the benefits of reading, make a habit of reading, be it one day a week; if it is possible for more days better and most importantly enjoy reading and what you read; In this way, you will get better use of fast and comprehensive reading.

I share some ideas for you to put into practice, as they will help you develop this habit, in addition to making reading a pleasant moment.

Read topics and cases that inspire

Regardless of your profession or specialty, reading positive topics will help you enjoy the time you spend.

Read about topics related to

- How to be optimistic about life.
- How to make friends.
- How to be happier
- Develop Emotional Intelligence
- Enjoy holidays in a village, on the beach.
- Personal stories and success stories little known.
- Personal image.
- How to overcome failures.
- How to acquire healthy habits.
- Inventions that have transformed the lives of people.
- Successful mindset

The list grows; the key is that these readings inspire in your life, in your professional activity and that motivates you to read more and more.

In addition, another reason to form the habit to read. Reading helps you open doors to connect with more people, in your growth

Read book summaries

If you are forming the habit by reading, reading condensates is a good option.

In addition to providing you with a global idea of the content, it will encourage you to know the detail of the work, facilitating understanding and speed reading.

The most appropriate hours for reading

When is it easier and more pleasant to read?

From experience, I tell you that the most convenient time to digest the book, magazine or favorite blog, changes from person to person; so if you do not feel comfortable right now, do not be discouraged.

Try different days, schedules.

The important thing is to find the best combination of 3 elements:

- Rapid reading techniques.
- Understanding what is read.
- Convert the habit by reading at a pleasant moment.

Generates an atmosphere of tranquility

This is a basic requirement in basic reading techniques,

setting the place of reading to facilitate concentration.

Although sometimes we find the title of a book or an interesting publication either in the bookstore, when browsing the internet in a public place, it is convenient that the environment is of tranquility.

Associate the moment to read with comfort and tranquility, that invites to enjoy reading and avoid distractions.

Take care of the lighting

The lack of lighting causes eyestrain, distractions or interruption of the material that is read.

Sometimes, the subject of reading is very interesting, we are very comfortable reading, we do not perceive the passing of the hours and that better lighting is necessary.

It is important to take care of the health, mainly of the eyes, reason why it is convenient to make a brief pause to turn on the lights of the room, of the table lamp or some lantern; In addition to take advantage to change your posture, sit down or get up a few minutes to activate circulation.

Use visual elements in the setting

More than decorations, use elements that motivate you to read. The phrases provide very good results.

They can be some like, "It's time to read," "A book awaits you," "Start now," or favorite motivational phrases.

I share phrases for improvement, which can be useful.

Do not vocalize.

This technique consists in abandoning the habit of repeating what is being read, known as vocalization.

What causes vocalize each word? Limit reading speed to speed to talk.

The speed to read is more linked to the speed of thought, so it is important to work on leaving behind this habit. The following exercise will help you with this.

Listen to music

When vocalizing, the attention of the mind is divided between what you read and the attention to your voice.

Taking the attention of the ears in something different helps to leave behind this habit.

Use appropriate music for concentration, which will help you focus your focus on reading. To reinforce the exercise, try to read faster than usual.

Remember, in addition to following and practicing quick reading techniques, it is important to understand them so that the material contributes value.

Alternate speeds

This is one of the quick reading techniques in which you will replace some practices that you learned in the early school stage. Especially since then you got used to reading word by word.

Amplify your vision

By developing the ability to expand your view of the material, it will allow you to absorb a greater number of words and increase reading speed.

What can be done to develop this capacity?

- How to read faster: Fast forward 2 or 3 words

If you are used to reading word by word, this is an exercise that will help you change.

With a support object, either a pencil or pen, point to the exact place you are reading; from there, your sight travels 2 or 3 words to the right.

The object of support allows to advance and read in a faster way. At the end of the line, amplify your vision by going diagonally to the next.

- Combine speed and understanding

Not all words require the same attention, words highlighted in bold, those that contain a technical vocabulary or those containing the main ideas, require a change at speed. The content that is more familiar can be read faster.

- Uses memorization and synthesis tricks
- Familiarize yourself with the acronyms

This is one of the quick reading techniques that require constant updating. They will allow you to focus attention on the material and avoid distractions by consulting external sources.

Some examples

- IMF - International Monetary Fund
- WHO - World Health Organization
- IOC - International Olympic Committee.

On the other hand with practice, you can group these words in their respective acronyms and move faster in reading.

Become familiar with the acronyms, as part of continuous learning. Use visual aids. The complication in understanding a topic hinders the progress of reading.

Is there any visual aid within the content?

For example, in technical issues, it is common to find graphs, tables with equivalences, formulas, as support material.

- Do not do reading marathons

Remember that your mind is not tireless after a certain time of concentration fatigue appears and the capacity for retention diminishes. In this state, there is no comprehensive reading.

It is better to intersperse periods of 40 minutes to one hour of reading, with a break. To divert the attention to another side after keeping the attention fixed on what is read is a rest for the sight.

Take advantage of rest breaks to change your position when sitting or walking to stretch your feet.

It is also an occasion to review other aspects as if there is still enough lighting, the temperature of the place is pleasant.

- Check details that may cause discomfort.

The discomfort is followed by distractions that can end with a quick reading session.

The practice will help you to improve the time of concentration, to enjoy reading for a longer time. Even so, do not forget these rest periods.

In the next section, I share exercises that will help you take advantage of these breaks to achieve better concentration.

Highlights key information

This is an important point in the understanding of reading. See the highlighted information in bold, the illustrations, the graphics. Identify valuable data, key information.

The graphs usually contain relevant data regarding behavior, evolution, trends, the focus of attention; that is, extract key information.

As mentioned earlier, this may mean reducing the reading speed. In return, you will be knowing and understanding arguments that contribute to your training and progress.

Do brain gymnastics

A relevant factor to read fast is concentration. Focusing the mind efficiently on the text, graphics, images, allows us to take advantage and advance with greater speed.

Within the techniques of rapid reading, the tools that contribute to having a better concentration stand out.

How to improve reading and concentration? Do brain gymnastics.

Brain fitness aims to improve brain performance and learning by performing physical exercises.

The exercises you can carry out before reading or even after a prolonged time of concentration will be very beneficial as it will clear your mind, preparing you to have better reasoning and awaken the creative side.

There are many exercises corresponding to this topic; I share 2 of them, which in addition to helping you improve concentration, you will enjoy practicing.

Movements using the fingers of the hands

It consists of exchanging movements using the fingers of the hands.

Initially, place the fingers of the hands as indicated previously, one hand with the thumb closed and the other 4 fingers open; with the other hand, keep your thumb open and closed the remaining 4 fingers.

Next, reverse the order. That is, the hand with which you initially had the four fingers open and the thumb closed, now closes the 4 fingers and opens the thumb. For the other hand, open the 4 fingers and close the thumb.

Repeat the exercise 5 to 10 times.

If the exercise is difficult, I share a trick. Invert the order of one hand first and then the other. However, the idea is to reverse the order of both hands at the same time.

Movements with arms

The next exercise consists of interspersing movements

with the arms.

As a first step, one of the arms is kept in the resting position. Lift the other arm so that it is stretched vertically and then bring it down in rest position. Repeat the movements with this arm 3 to 5 times, so that the routine is recorded in the mind.

As a second step, the arm that was in motion passes to the rest position. Stretch the other arm at shoulder height horizontally and out of the body; Now stretch it up vertically; return to the stretched horizontal position and then bring it down to the rest position. Repeat the movements with this arm 3 to 5 times, too, so that the routine is recorded in the mind.

Next, simultaneously perform the first and second steps, in such a way that both arms perform their respective routines, step 1 and steps 2 at the same time, from 5 to 10 times.

This point allows you to ensure that you are assimilating the content you are reading.

I share the following exercises that will help you.

- Make your own summaries

One of the purposes of reading is to obtain profit, apply it daily and in the professional aspect, as well as having arguments to make decisions.

It will not help you to learn to read fast if you do not

remember its content afterward.

To learn quick reading techniques, you must decide how conscientiously you need to understand the material you have available.

More than understanding word by word, it is more important to highlight the main ideas.

It prepares summaries of the content read, as well as verifies the understanding of it.

I recommend you carry out the following.

- Highlights the relevant points
- Underline the main ideas. The advantages that this action offers you is to highlight the main ideas. They will also be useful for later consultation. This, you can also do it in electronic readings.
- Ask questions. What have you learned? This is a way to follow the understanding of reading
- Share the knowledge
- Verify what you have learned, sharing with others. So, talk to your closest friends about the knowledge gathered recently.
- When you share the material that you have read, you will reinforce the domain of the topic and can inspire others to be interested in the topic
- Another advantage is that you can find affinity in other people. That is, those who share with

you the passion for reading and even for the topics of your interest. This will allow bouncing ideas and even learn more.

Conclusions

There are quick reading techniques that allow you to double or triple the reading speed. This allows you to absorb more knowledge with less effort; Enjoy the time spent reading and consuming more content.

In the business world, reading faster helps to optimize the agenda while being updated and aware of opportunities and even some threats.

The purpose of this section is to find a balance between speed and understanding of the material read.

It does not help much to break records of speed per minute or per page if you do not enjoy yourself or do not read with a purpose. It does not help much knowing a number of quick reading techniques if you do not have the habit to read.

Increase speed and learn to read faster, start with making the decision to work for this purpose. However, remember that in addition to achieve this change, that reading is a pleasant time and increase the understanding of the material, the value you will get from this process will be even more profitable.

It is then, time to apply these techniques of rapid reading and understanding to continue growing and generate opportunities.

Speed Reading Techniques For Effective Reading

Learning speed reading techniques are being embraced by more and more people like the benefits of it are widely understood. It can be defined as a skill which enables a person to read at an accelerated pace without greatly reducing the retention and comprehension levels.

Why Should One Learn Speed Reading Techniques?

People try to improve all the other skills, but often ignore reading skills. Students and research scholars, who are required to read a huge chunk of materials on a daily basis, can effectively benefit from learning speed reading techniques. By enhancing their reading speed, students can cover more chapters compared to their contemporaries and can find more time to study other subjects. It is proved that children who are blessed with the skill often outperform in their studies. Since it's techniques also enhance retention capability, one will be able to recall the vital matters without re-reading the text.

Speed reading skill will also help employees in the corporate world to read and comprehend reports, emails, newspapers, correspondences and technical papers faster. Since they are required to be up-to-date with new information without sacrificing the office duties, speed reading techniques will prove to be helpful. These techniques that help to manage reading and comprehension at an accelerated rate will lead to increased productivity and efficiency. Communication skills and personality will also be improved, along with assisting you in finding time for other important stuff in life.

There are a whole lot of courses that teach different skills based on a collection of methods and techniques. These courses are available in the form of books, videos, software, and seminars.

Speed Reading Techniques

Learning to increase the speed at which you read, of course, won't increase your Iq, but it will increase your brain's ability to comprehend new concepts.

In order to master the fast reading skill, one must be a good reader. The reader's knowledge of vocabulary should be strong if he/she wants to comprehend the stuff fast. If one's vocabulary and comprehension are strong enough, the technique will be of much help in mastering the skill.

Avoid Word By Word Reading

Reading word by word is a poor reading habit, and unfortunately, this is how children are traditionally taught to read and learn. Overcoming this habit will itself enhance a person's reading ability. The problem with word by word reading is that the reader will fail to comprehend the overall concept in the text, as he/she will be focusing on separate words. The techniques deal with reading chunks or blocks of a word at a time and grasping the essence of those word groups. Once you learn to read more words in a block and comprehend, the faster you will read. The best way to hold the book is to keep it a little further from your eyes.

Avoid Sub-Vocalization

A clinical term for pronouncing each word while reading, sub-vocalization will reduce the speed and comprehension ability. The reason is that when you read put each word louder; you will first hear the word spoken leading to the slow down of the comprehension process. Practicing reading until you get rid of this habit is the only way out.

Read While You Read

Eliminating multi-tasking while reading will help in improving the speed at which you read. Try to avoid all disturbances and distractions from the place where you sit and read.

Skim the Content for Main Ideas

Stop considers reading as a linear practice. Try to avoid sequential reading by taking in every word, sentence, paragraph, page, and chapter in order, which will divert your attention to supplementary and superfluous materials. Scan the text and focus on the vital content. Look for bullet points or things in bold. Skim the text to avoid the fluff and concentrate on the key material.

Take Breaks

Reading steadily for hours together will affect the reading efficiency and will slow down the process of retention. Take specific time breaks to refresh yourself and to avoid overstraining your eyes.

Remember that for acquiring the skill there is no magic formula. Practicing with full concentration is the only way to master this valuable art.

How To Use Cold Reading To Seduce

The cold reading is often used by magicians, psychics, seers, to find details about a person and make you believe that they know more about you than you can imagine. Typical sentences may look like: Have you had a promotion recently? or again: I feel that you have an artist's soul. The cold reading allows knowing everything about your subject in record time, provided to practice and gain experience: this is what is also called to manipulation. However, this is an area that can be used easily in seduction and that's what we're going to study now.

Seduction And Manipulation

In our societies, we are all manipulated, that it is your mother when you were small: if you do not finish your plate you will not be able to play! but also your boss at the office: I want your report on the table as of Friday, or you can forget your promotion. In an ideal society, there would be no manipulation. But that's how our societies were built, so maybe it's time to know how to counter it or how to use it.

The Basic Procedure

First of all, you have to start the discussion with the person you want to seduce. Once it's trusted and relaxed, you'll be able to use your Cold Reader capabilities. With this technique, you can make it feel like you know a lot more about herself than any other person in the room.

The main idea is to use a large number of questions and affirmations (coming from the techniques mentioned below in this section) and to adjust them according to the answers or the behavior of the person. For example, when you just fall and say something to a person (I'm sure you're Dutch!), the person will probably look more interested; widen his eyes or respond with a big yes while he did not say anything before.

It is, therefore, necessary to analyze his facial behavior, his body language, his answers, etc., a large number of criteria that will help you to take certain directions during your next questions. This can be added to Warm Reading, which is to collect information from other sources, such as getting information from friends or seeing photos of the house, etc.

This is done without having talked about it beforehand. Imagine the effect: You are in law school, license II, I felt it in your way of speaking, when in fact the information was taken from a relative of the subject.

An Example Of Approach Thanks To Cold Reading

As with cold reading, we are often mistaken in the statements we give, we must always think about minimizing mistakes and put forward claims that are right, because the subject will not hold and will be interested only to these. This will give the impression to the person that we really know it. The human being quickly forgets the false statements, which increases the effect of this technique.

For example, during a TV show with a medium, it has managed to read in the past of the various topics on the board. The participants reviewed the recording the next day and realized after the fact that the medium had only one statement just about ten established. Despite this, during the show, the participants really felt that his gift was real.

The Technique Of Cold Reading Shotgunning

This technique of cold reading is often used by mediums on television. It bears this particular name because it consists of analyzing the subject with several small affirmations rather than with a single general statement. It is enough to project on the subject, a large number of vague suppositions.

We have not met before? You were there with a friend at a party, or rather a boy, or your boyfriend? It was a few weeks ago, maybe a little more. No wait, it was not long ago.

The Barnum Effect

This cold reading technique is named after the famous Phineas Taylor Barnum, an American show entrepreneur. It consists of exposing quite personal affirmations, whereas, in fact, they apply to every one according to the personality traits that each one attributes to himself, considering himself as universally good. During the reading of these sentences, it is necessary to study the reactions of the person to know which subjects will be reactive or not and to adapt the continuation according to these reactions.

Here is the example of the famous psychologist, Bertram r. Forer

You need to be loved and admired, and yet you are too critical of yourself. You have weaknesses in your personality, but you usually know how to compensate for them. You have considerable potential that you have not used to your advantage yet. Outside you are disciplined and you know how to control yourself, but inside you tend to be concerned and not very sure of yourself. Sometimes you seriously wonder if you made the right decision or did what needed to be done to overcome the difficulties in your life. You prefer a certain amount of change and variety and become dissatisfied if you are surrounded by restrictions and limitations. You flatter yourself to be an independent spirit and you accept the opinion of others only if it is brilliantly demonstrated. But you found that it was awkward to reveal yourself too easily to others. At times you are very extroverted, talkative and sociable, while at other times you are introverted and reserved. Some of your aspirations tend to be quite unrealistic but you are a dreamer and tend to have a lot of ambition, that's a good thing.

Almost any of these phrases can be used during a party, or drift slightly depending on your subject's reaction.

The Cold Reading Technique Called The Cunning Rainbow

The ruse rainbow consists of saying everything and its opposite in the same sentence. A person has several character traits that can be described but in an unquantifiable way.

An Example Of The Cunning Rainbow Technique

I know that you are someone shy inside you, even if in society you seem to have confidence in you. You are an admirable person with your friends and someone you can count on, but if someone breaks that trust then you are capable of the worst anger.

The cold reader can put a character trait and its opposite in the same sentence, connecting everything by a mood, or a moment.

Cold Reading Thanks To The Barnum Effect

Also called "Drill Effect", the Barnum effect is what is most used in the field of Cold Reading. This will allow your subject to accept a vague description of himself as being a truth that applies specifically to him. In this way, the person will feel that you know a lot about her when in reality, you only flatter her ego: flattery that many will assimilate as being a specific and individual truth, so a truth, in short, that they will accept without asking questions. For you, the effect Barnum is an open door on your subject, who will be more able to deliver information about him, thinking he has no secrets for you.

The psychologist B.G. Forer explained the results of this effect in terms of human credulity, vanity and a tendency to make sense. Thus, people feel more easily concerned with proposals if they have the desire that these proposals are true, even if they correspond to them in a vague way. The subjects thus find a way to confirm their hopes and expectations.

The Barnum Effect In Our Society

It is assumed that the Barnum effect comes into play in certain specific situations. For example, recognizing oneself in the personality tests found in many magazines. This can also be the case with a horoscope or a horoscope.

But it is certainly during a clairvoyance consultation that the Barnum effect has the strongest influence. Indeed, the information given by the indicator is directly addressed to the person. According to the results of Forer, a person will, therefore, tend to recognize himself in what the witness says, even if the information given is vague and general, and even more so if these descriptions correspond to the expectations of the person who comes to consult.

However caution, it does not make it possible to determine if clairvoyance is reducible to the Barnum Effect, but its knowledge makes it possible to be a little more cautious on the interpretations delivered by this type of interaction.

What Are The Five Received Ideas Of Cold Reading

Have you heard of Cold Reading, but do not know exactly what it is? Some people have told you about it but you are still not convinced?

It is normal, cold reading is a field of study of the psyche rather difficult to assimilate at the beginning, but it is with training and experience that you will arrive at your ends. However, before you even start practicing in the field, you need to know the five most popular ideas on cold reading, to get around them and study without making mistakes.

I - Nonverbal Language And Cold Reading

Many people think that cold reading is based on the client's non-verbal language: facial expressions, position, manner, and gestures. Nonverbal language may play a role, indeed, but a minor one. It will serve, for example, to support one of your theories or suggestions on the subject, and will confirm or not them. He can not, for example, help during a cold reading by phone, or in writing. Moreover, nonverbal language can not be used for "psychic" readings containing names, dates, or details about the subject's past.

II - Deduction Of Information And Cold Reading

Some skeptics think that the cold reader uses information inference to get clues about the client's character, interests, and career. This technique is also used in cold reading. However, this is not the most important because sometimes it is unusable like when a cold reading is done on the radio, on the phone, or by mail. The potential for information deduction is in reality very limited. However, even admitting that deductive observation can sometimes work very well, cold reading is not primarily used to provide accurate information, but to make it seem like a strategy, that we know a lot about a person, when in fact we know very little about it at all.

III - Fishing For Clues And Cold Reading

Another popular theory is that cold reading is just fishing for clues. There is a background of truth in this because the reader can use subtle tricks to obtain the desired information. However, fishing for clues is only a small part of the explanation of cold reading and everything lies in how to get the information and then use it.

IV - Imprecision And Generalization

Some people think that a "psychic" reading consists exclusively of vague and generalized statements that could mean almost anything. However, you will be able to realize that this is false. Many cold readers give their client-specific information, such as names, dates, and detailed descriptions of people and places.

V - Stupid, Gullible And Naive

Finally, there are those who think that those who will consult clairvoyants, psychics, etc., must be stupid, credulous or naive. This is an assertion that is totally contrary to the facts because countless very intelligent and very insightful clients consult for a psychic reading. If you know what cold reading is if you know how it works and the different ways to parry it then it can not be used on you, while if it does not, it can, whatever your level of intelligence or your intellectual abilities. None of these qualities present difficulties for a good cold reader.

Learn Cold Reading

Remember, cold reading is a very difficult area and it's not just about reading to get there, but you also need to understand the meaning of the parts. Now that you are up to date on the five received ideas, you will be able to work around some mistakes not to be made, and some prejudices to avoid.

16 questions to Know a Person's Personality

We do not always know people as much as we think. Sometimes they show only the side they want you to see. Knowing this, the question arises: are there questions to know the personality of a person?

The answer is yes! By asking the right questions, you can better identify the traits and characteristics of each one. Want to know how? Check it out!

How important is it to ask questions to know a person's personality?

The questions to know the personality of a person need to be made naturally and flow during the conversation. This is because it is important not to let the other person feel pressured.

Knowing one's personality before even living is ideal in many cases, especially in the work environment, since good living together is ideal for business to flow.

In addition, it is important that the profiles are compatible. Even seeking diversity and new perceptions, it is necessary to have individuals who are engaged in the cause, focused and committed to the work.

Therefore, it is ideal to ask these 16 questions to know the personality of a person:

1. What are your hobbies?

2. What is your greatest passion?

3. What is your biggest dream?

4. What is your greatest fear?

5. What is your favorite book or movie?

6. What did you want to be when you were little?

7. How do you think your parents would describe you?

8. Do you consider yourself a happy person?

9. Which event in your life has most marked you?

10. What are your greatest qualities and defects?

11. Would you change anything about yourself? What would it be?

12. What is the quality of someone else that pleases you most?

13. How do you deal with a colleague you do not like?

14. How do you cope with stress at work?

15. What would you still like to learn?

16. If you only have one more day to live, what would you do?

From them, it is possible to identify behavioral and psychological aspects, identifying the way the person sees himself and how he sees the world.

Thus, it is also possible to understand the perceptions and what the individual expects from others, identifying their frustrations, fears, conquests, needs, and desires. It is even a viable means for creating people in the professional environment, for example.

However, it is important to remember that we should not go beyond limits or force the other to respond to anything that is not comfortable. The denials also have a lot to say about the profile of the individual.

Did you like to know how to get to know your friend, family or neighbor better? Put these questions into practice and see how you might be surprised!

THE MOST EFFECTIVE TECHNIqUES TO USE EMOTIONAL MANIPULATION, AT WORK, IN A RELATIONSHIP AND IN LIFE IN GENERAL

The technique of manipulating through emotional confusion is definitely the most popular one and is pretty easy to do. It basically plays on eliminating logic from the conversation. Logic allows the person to think and the last thing you want your target to do is to think because it can block or prevent basic manipulation. What you want to do is steer the conversation to a place where he or she is in an emotional state so their ability to think rationally is severely diminished.

A lot of people think that emotional manipulation is all about constantly invoking strong emotional states to remove logic from the situation. This is only partly true, you have to choose the right moment to invoke that strong emotional surge! If you constantly switch between strong emotional states it will only confuse your target and actually prevent you from implementing your ideas.

This is where emotional control comes in, most of the time you have to keep your emotions in check, don't react, stay cool and friendly (I call this being the grounded friend). This is harder than you might think as your mind has the constant urge to react to every impulse that enters the brain! The goal is to stay friendly always and forever right up to the point where the manipulation starts, being likable creates trust and prevents doubt!

But the real power in being the grounded friend all the time lies in how others will see you, they will see a very confident and down-to-earth person who is in total control of his life. This means that you'll almost always have the upper hand in conversations as your confidence outshines theirs... this will work on 60% of all people! It is however very important that you don't get cocky as this will break the illusion!

You might ask what to do with the other 40%? well, 10% of them are the alpha types, high in confidence but a lot of them are slightly less intelligent... which means they are easier to manipulate with logic! The other 30% are the tricky ones, this is where the real power of being always cool or friendly comes in... When you seem grounded all the time then the moments where you actually show strong emotions have an enormous impact! The impact is so big that even the tricky 30% will be fooled into thinking you're for real, this is why you do it, this is why you keep your emotions in check... because when you actually show emotions, people will notice and believe almost anything you say at this point!

Keep in mind that these tips can also be used to recognize situations where you are the one being manipulated!

Business Success Is All About Emotional Connections

When I walk into a new business to teach selling, they expect... Sales techniques... Tricks... Manipulation 101.

But that's not what works today in selling! We have all sorts of research showing that people hate to feel manipulated or tricked, and move away from manipulators!

So what's working in selling... and, for that matter, in all aspects of business success? Positive emotional connections!

In 2002, Dr. Daniel Kahneman, a Psychology professor at Princeton, won the Nobel Prize for economics. His studies proved that we behave emotionally first, and rationally second.

quoting author Susan Scott in her book *Fierce Leadership*, "We are emotional beings engaged in emotional enterprises. Without an emotional impetus, we withhold our best efforts, drag our feet, delay decisions, or walk away altogether. The competition offers a better price, and 'loyal' customer leave. Talented, unengaged employees learn of a work environment in which they sense they'll be happier, and they, too, will be gone."

"This is not hypothetical," she concludes. "The lack of meaningful connections with coworkers and customers is costing companies billions annually."

I'm struck that this insight is not more respected - more top-of-mind and a part of strategic thinking. Yet as I go from company to company consulting, the importance of emotional connections is just not being discussed.

There is always an emotional aspect of complex sales.

Even when the purchase is high-tech, even when those doing the purchasing are highly rational, there's a rational part of the buying process - that's what gets you and your offering considered. And then there's the emotional part - and that's what leads to your being chosen over others, all of whom could have done the work.

So what would happen differently if you told yourself that your sales - or even your career - depend on emotional connections and emotional decision-making?

- Would you, perhaps, stop relying on data to "make the case" for working with you? And would you think more about the specific individuals who are making the decision, and what's driving them? (Would you be open to "drivers" that are not logical?)
- Might you, perhaps, stop sending emailed proposals, trusting that the logic in the document will get you selected, and, instead, spend more time face-to-face and phone-to-phone with those who can choose to spend money with you? (Research says such "F2F and P2P time" correlates directly with closed sales. We have no comparable data for E2E - email to email communication).
- Could you focus more on the words people use, rather than just the underlying concepts they're communicating, seeking the emotional loading on their conversations, and even their emails?

All are changes for the better.

Sales Techniques - Effectively Using Neuro-linguistic Programming To Sell More

There are many kinds of sales techniques that make use of neuro-linguistic programming. Clearly defined, NLP is the study of experiences and beliefs and their effect on the words that people choose to use when they speak.

It is these very same influences that are being used in order to use NLP for sales. There are many different types of small things that one can do in order to make the most of what the person is feeling as of the moment, as well as the things that they have experienced in the past.

NLP has to be properly, though not formally, studied in order for one to be able to use it properly to improve certain sales techniques.

This is because the brain is probably the most complex thing about the human being, and while there are many studies about this kind of manipulation technique, the inclusion of external stimuli, as well as the fact that each and every person has an individual personality and experience, makes it that much harder to generalize human beings and the words that they use.

The difference between the brains of men and women is a prime example of this. Men and women use their brains differently, but this is also just a broad generalization.

In general, women respond to more emotional stimuli, whereas men respond more to visual stimuli. This is one of the reasons why men are more particular about how their partner looks than women are.

The approach that one must take then is through the words that he or she must use when speaking to the potential customer or client.

Sales techniques such as these are more commonly used by people who spend a lot of time speaking with their clients or customers before making a sale, such as people who sell for insurance companies, real estate and the like.

What you can do then is to use certain words that will trigger emotions in them. Generally what you want your potential client to feel first and foremost is trust both in your as someone who is trying to sell them something, as well as in the product that you are trying to sell to them.

The words you can use then are words that will trigger in them an emotion of need, whether for them alone or for them and their family. Once you have been able to point out that they have a certain need, you then point out that your product is that which will be the one to fulfill that need.

This is one of the more simplistic examples of sales

techniques that use neuro-linguistic programming, but you get a general idea. The way for you to be able to perfect this then is to keep on practicing it, either by going through training or simply by experience.

Another basic principle of NLP for use in sales techniques is to make the most of the five senses. These five senses are basically how each and every human being takes in and perceives the world, either just one or a combination of the five.

When you use these five senses in order to show your client just how good your product will be for them, they will begin to see things in that light due to the fact that all five of their senses are telling them so.

So if you need new and innovative sales techniques, do not hesitate to study more about neuro-linguistic programming. All you have to do is to understand how it truly works, and you will be able to use it for the benefit of your product and your company.

Persuasion and Manipulation in Sales

Both persuasion and manipulation are methods of convincing people to do something, react favorably to your ideas or change their thinking to match yours. They are based on some principles of human action and interaction. Though the two are similar to some extent, they follow different styles and their results are usually different.

Salesperson's job is to persuade people, however careless adoption of persuasion techniques may lead to the concept of manipulation. Salespeople should understand the two concepts and try to avoid using manipulation to make sales. Here are some of the differences between them.

Persuasion is ethical while manipulation is not.

Persuasion is about influencing people about something they need. On the other hand, manipulation is about convincing people about something you want. A well-executed persuasion will build loyalty and trust from your customers resulting in repeat purchases. Though manipulation can build trust and loyalty as well, it will only be short-termed and will be followed by permanent detachment. Forceful persuasion is manipulation and you should avoid it.

The aim of manipulation is to control. Using manipulation will result in win and loss situations. Sometimes you will make sales and other times your targets will outsmart you and fail to make any purchases. In contrast to manipulation, persuasion aims at boosting the self-esteem of the target customers. It involves treating them well and showing them respect. This will result in the target customers reacting positively to your offers.

When trying to make a sale you should ask questions to understand your customer's situation. You need to be open and present the facts of your products in a positive light and show how they will benefit the users. This is what persuasion is all about. Manipulation, on the other hand, involves playing with the emotions of other parties and leaving out useful information. Manipulators normally imply and make up nonexistent facts.

Manipulation is self-centered. A manipulator only does what he feels is beneficial to himself and doesn't care if someone gets hurt in the process. This is a bad business practice which will end up losing all your customers.

Persuasion aims to serve. A persuader knows the importance of his customers and aims at taking their interests at heart. A persuader builds strong and long-lasting relationships with his customers.

While both manipulators and persuaders understand the importance of motivation in influencing decision making, manipulators use this knowledge to their advantage while persuaders use it to the advantage of their customers.

An understanding of these concepts is very important to every salesperson. Effective persuasion techniques will result in favorable responses from your targets. However, though manipulation will help you make some sales, it is usually damaging in the long-run and you should avoid it at all costs. An understanding of persuasion techniques will not only increase your sales, but it will also help grow strong bonds with your customers, thus, winning their trust and loyalty.

Mind Control Techniques - Making People Do What You Want

You probably think it is impossible, but you can learn and master different mind control techniques.

These are powerful tools for making others do what you want them to. There are a lot of ways in which you can be a good manipulator, but it is best to focus on the best ones. Learn more about the most effective mind control techniques.

Love bombing might sound weird, but it is a particularly simple and effective method for manipulation. It is one of the mind control techniques that have been tested and proven to work.

As the name suggests, your task is to make the person

you want to control like you and feel comfortable around you through making him feel loved. There are different stages that this technique involves. You have to start by flattering the person so that he immediately likes you.

Then you can focus on building empathy in your relationship. This is best done by sharing your emotions and secrets (not the real ones, though). You have to be on the same wavelength as the person. Make him feel that you like the same things and share the same ideas.

The physical contact is extremely important for the success of this one of the mind control techniques. You can readily give the person a warm hug when he needs it or holds his hand during a tough moment.

Provided that you are doing everything correctly, the person you want to manipulate will think of you as family. This will allow you to influence him effectively. This person will be prepared to do everything for you.

Rejection of old values is another one of the effective mind control techniques. The key goal here is to change the way to thinking of the person so that you can make him more submissive to your suggestions.

You have to focus on renouncing the existing values of the person. This takes time and effort, but you will accomplish it with persistence.

You have to start with renouncing the beliefs of the person. This can be easily done through questioning. In this way, the person will feel that he has reached the conclusion by himself.

Then, you can work on the actual rejection of old values. The best way to accomplish success is to replace them with new ones.

For example, if a person thinks that what matters most is having fun, you can readily convince him that what matters the most is friendship (and your friendship, in particular).

Once you have transformed the person using this one of the mind control techniques, you can focus on making him do what you want. Use the rejection of the old values and the acceptance of new ones as your weapons.

Covert hypnosis is another one of the mind control techniques that work brilliantly. It is more straightforward than the other two, even though it involves the use of a variety of sub-techniques.

The main advantage of using this method is that you can apply it on anyone, even strangers, easily and quickly.

Covert hypnosis is achieved during the course of a seemingly traditional conversation. It has three main stages - building rapport with the subject, reaching his subconscious mind and making subliminal messages.

You can use both love bombing and the rejection of old values as part of this method. The first one of the mind control techniques is effective for building rapport, making the subject like you.

You can readily use the physical touch masterfully for reaching the subconscious mind of the subject as well.

The value rejection of mind control techniques can be used for creating confusion. This can be particularly effective for switching off the critical mind and influencing the subconscious one.

Once the person is in the state of trance, you can readily make the suggestions, subliminal messages. At this point, you have to say what you want the other person to do. If you are talking to a pretty girl that you want to ask out, you simply have to say, "Go out with me". She will.

These mind control techniques have been tested and proven to work. You should definitely devote time and effort to mastering them. Keep learning and practicing to make others do what you want them to.

HOW TO USE MANIPULATION TO SEDUCTION

One Powerful Trick of Manipulation and Seduction That You Can Use Today!

Dale Carnegie was a self-made businessman that wrote the still best selling "How to Win Friends and Influence People." Read by millions of people this self-help book has transformed lives around the world. The core of this popular self-help book is ten principles to use to influence and persuade others to go along with your idea.

One of these techniques can be powerfully used to seduce and make them think it was their idea to leave the bar, and the safety of their friends to a hotel room with you. Sound far-fetched? Well, when you use this powerful technique properly she will open up her mind and her heart to you and your ideas, allowing you to penetrate areas she only keeps reserved for a long-standing boyfriend.

This technique has been proven again and again in various social experiments and written up in various journals of psychology. The technique is to assign a label to her, a label that she would likely enjoy having. Like being adventurous, or being kind, or being smart.

And then when you suggest subsequent ideas to her, frame them so that if she agrees to them, she will get to keep the positive label. If she refuses, then she loses the label.

For example, let's say through conversation, you get her to admit that she is adventurous and likes to have fun. Most people would agree to these two labels. You can get her to say this by asking her some fun things she's done in the past. Then while she is telling you the story, say something like "Wow, you sound like a really fun adventurous person." After she agrees, and finish her story, ask her for more examples of her doing fun and adventurous stuff. This way she will participate in solidifying these two labels.

Then when it's time to leave, or when you want to leave, look around and something like this:

"You, most people aren't like you. Most people aren't very fun or adventurous. Some will say that they are, but they are really just saying that to make themselves look good. For example, most people wouldn't be adventurous enough to go on a date with somebody that they just met. They'd rather do the boring, safe thing, and need to be introduced by friends or something."

You can try this or some variation of this. The more you practice it, the better it will work. Of course, you always need to maintain your integrity. If you do this to manipulate somebody against their will or get somebody to do something they will later regret, you will suffer in the long run.

Because this technique is so powerful and taps a deep need for human nature to be consistent, it can be easily abused to make people do things they've would never consider under normal circumstances. Many people have used this technique and others for their own benefit, without concern for others. And the results have always been disastrous.

Seduction has a dark side. A side that some even willingly use to destroy. Find out what transformed such a shy, conservative churchgoer into a powerfully irresistible seducer of women, with horrible consequences.

Seduction

The art of eloquence in seduction

In this section, we wanted to address the question of eloquence in the particular field of seduction. How to apply the art of eloquence to seduction? How to use good communication techniques to make beautiful encounters? How to put eloquence into practice, i.e. how to express oneself with ease but also the art of moving, in one's emotional life?

Here I will share here many of these secrets and give us the best advice to use the force of eloquence in the context of a report of seduction:

Some politicians, journalists or media lawyers have the ability to speak in public with such confidence and confidence that it is sometimes surprising. In seduction, it is a bit the same principle. When you approach a person with the goal of getting an appointment or simply creating a link, the words you are going to speak, as well as the way you will behave, are paramount.

1. Target your line of work immediately

As in all areas, eloquence can be worked on and of course improved through specific work, ideally as part of coaching or coaching.

Even if the goal is to seduce more effectively, there are plenty of points to work on. The art of effective dialogue is not only acquired through the enrichment of vocabulary. You have to know what to say, to have the words to say it, but especially to know how to say it - to find the right tone, to join the good gesture ... There are many areas on which the work can be focused, and which are therefore likely to lead to improve your seduction game. It goes without saying that knowing as many words as you can is useful, but it's not the only factor to consider. The eloquence in seduction is also being able to manage the details that can have major importance: the voice and posture.

To develop your eloquence and especially to apply each of these tips to your seduction, I invite you to determine a specific line of work. It is essential to advance by small objectives in order to take control of your evolution. Determine immediately: "What is your first axis of development?"

2. Exercise to set up immediately

The next time you are in front of someone you might want to seduce, I ask you to think about standing up straight, keeping your shoulders open, and not letting your eyes fall or run down. This position will allow you to gain in charisma and therefore better convey your speech. Try to reproduce it with at least 3 interlocutors during the day. You will see that when you are less right and your eyes are fleeing, your interlocutor does not give you the same attention!

Why seduction is a field apart?

I imagine that in your opinion, eloquence is only a question of practice and you are half right. In reality, there are so many parameters to master that practice can not solve everything. In addition, you can perfectly be very eloquent in a specific area, but when you find yourself in another context, you lose your footing. It is clear that seduction is an integral part of these "separate" areas where stress management is a central issue.

In front of a person whom you appreciate, it will be more difficult to keep your natural, to be really spontaneous, and that is why I invite you to work on your personal confidence.

In seduction, if you take confidence in yourself, you will be able to overcome your blockages and thus to approach the person who really attracts you!

To develop your eloquence in seduction, I first invite you to learn to communicate better with all the people around you and develop your ability to "socialize". You can only take advantage of this experience to be more comfortable in all your relationships, establish new links and promote beautiful meetings, including dating.

- Exercise to set up to seduce quickly

Take a few minutes in your day to approach 3 unknown people. The main objective is to dialogue and to attract attention. If you are able to interest strangers then you can easily seduce people who attract you!

- Eloquence and seduction, details to know!

Eloquence in seduction is not (only) to use nice words or to make pretty sentences, because the risk is to pass for a talker and you probably know that by acting in this way you risk to not be able to conclude.

In reality, the art of communicating is much broader and you should not just focus on the word. It is essential to take several parameters into consideration, especially body language, which allows you to establish an immediate connection with your contact person.

- Exercise to do immediately

When speaking with someone, do not hesitate to touch your elbow 3 times during your conversation ("cubital tunnel" technique). You will realize that the connection is created quickly and that your power of seduction is reinforced!

Your strategy of seduction is partly based on your eloquence. Everything is not only based on the physical, nor on the fact of having woven a social link prior to the meeting. And even if it does, the fact of better communicating with your interlocutor can only be an additional advantage. With your new way of communicating, you will not go unnoticed. You will release this essential magnetism when you want to attract a person, and that will allow you to be immediately noticed by the one you want to charm. Your words and your attitude will now be your best assets!

DEFINE AND OPTIMIZE YOUR MESSAGES, ALTERS THEIR PERCEPTION

Coercive Persuasion And Modification Of Behavior, Attitudes, And Emotions

The mental manipulation is the set of maneuvers to change the decision-making processes of an individual or a social group and by the use of individual, physical or psychological techniques (psychological) to the place under the partial or total control of the author of the manipulation. Faced with this definition is the problem of the degree of manipulation - socially acceptable or morally and ethically reprehensible.

Mental manipulation techniques have evolved greatly and have greatly refined in recent decades and have reached unprecedented sophistication. It presents itself on a continuum of strategies. Advances in psychology in neuropsychology have made it possible to implement, with a certain degree of refinement, strategies of persuasion and manipulations, which are distinct from folklore (a picturesque, but superficial and meaningless manifestation) that is often conveyed and often rude; such as the one where one finds people to go, attach, undergo electric shocks and receiving injections. It is now possible to use a set of strategies, very subtle, very clean, that fit into everyday life.

The coercion is defined as the fact of "hold or constrain by force." Legally this often involves the use of physical force or physical or legal threats. The technical concepts of "coercive persuasion", which are effectively restrictive, debilitating or restrictive by the gradual application of psychological forces.

The coercive persuasion is a technique of social influence capable of producing substantial changes in behavior and attitudes that are applied to cause "learning" and "the social normalization" by coercive tactics, persuasion and/or manipulative group and/or interpersonal influence. It is characterized by the conditions under which it is practiced and by the environmental and interpersonal manipulation techniques used to suppress particular behaviors or beliefs to lead others. The coercive persuasion or "thought reform" can be defined as a coordinated system of coercive influence and behavioral control designed to manipulate and deceive an individual in the interest of the author.

So we define the thought reform as a belief change in adapting to situations (loss of the locus of control). The elements which allow the distinction to other schemas of socialization are the mental manipulation, the psychological and interpersonal attack to disturb the notion of personal identity and the Self (social identity), the use of an organized group of pairs and interpersonal pressure, which enhances the value of conformity; the handling and control of the whole of the environment of the subject aim to stabilize behavioral changes. This control is carried out by people or group entities interposed on the places frequented by the target.

The coercive persuasion reports attempts to force a targeted person to change their beliefs, ideas, attitudes or behaviors, and using psychological pressure, to abuse of influence, abuse of authority and power, threats, anxiety, intimidation and/or stress. The coercive persuasion can be seen in many organizations and group entity - some public schools and universities, aggressive sales organizations, etc.

The Coercive persuasion raises attempts to overcome critical thinking and informed decision. Critical thinking, emotional defenses, cognitive thinking, values, ideas, relationships, attitudes, and behaviors are compromised by hypnotic communication, threat strategies and disguised bullying. As a result of the imposition of disguised coercive strategies, a person becomes incapable of making rational, enlightened decisions, and/or can not criticize or perceive the value, ideas or dogmas that are submitted to him or imposed.

The social control coercive persuasion is characterized by the control of communication, emotional and behavioral manipulation; compliance with derivative or deviant behavior; solicitations for confessions; the manipulation of language by clichés; finally, the reinterpretation of emotion and human experience (redefinition of the person's experience) and the feeling of inferiority experienced by those subjected to this technique. To belong to the group, the target must model its behavior on that of others. This imitation erases his individuality and his personal identity. By replacing the indecisions born of free will by automatic conduct, imitation exacerbates conformity and submission. Illustrated by Milgram's experiments, it is a question of obeying without reserve a recognized or proclaimed authority.

The essential strategy used by such techniques is to systematically select a sequence and continuously coordinate the many tactics of coercive persuasion over extended periods of time. Thought reform strategies are sophisticated and subtle, creating a psychological attachment or dependency that is far more powerful than a threat- only methods of influence. The psychological destabilization successful product a negative shift in the overall assessments of self (loss of self-esteem) and increases uncertainty about individual values and positions (loss of landmarks). Psychological and moral violence destabilizes and weakens the individual, weakens critical thinking and psychological defenses, thus making him available for the suggestion, manipulation, and persuasion, as well as establishing a dominant relationship / dominated.

In this way, it substantially reduces resistance to requests for objectivity while increasing suggestibility (a subject that is easy to influence by suggestion). In a three-phase model, the period of destabilization will be followed by a phase of "change" leading to a consolidation stage of "reform" and strengthening of thought.

The procedures of influence can be used during interrogations (the physician psychiatrist) can manipulate the beliefs of people on their own "innocence" (by guilt or exacerbation of latent guilt) and, in this way, lead them to confess a "crime" (guilty of deviance) that they did not commit. Confessions resulting from the successful application of phases of the sequential model of thought reform are classified as "forced and internalized" false confessions. The use of certain interrogation procedures creates a psychological vulnerability (which can be exacerbated by latent guilt) minimum in the "suspect", which is enough to obtain a confession of this "suspect" confession to which this "suspect" himself believes.

Misleading communication takes different forms and serves different purposes. The dissimulation , exaggeration (amplifying) the equivocal (location, expression is not clear, which can be interpreted in different ways), half-lies , the pretense (pretense, false appearance) the claim (or irony), the cartoon (rough representation, unfaithful to reality), these rhetorical devices (sophism art of discourse; all processes and techniques to express themselves eloquently, to convince, to persuade) can all be considered as types of misleading communication.

The simulation mechanisms might be involved in a large number of other mental processes as contradictory reasoning or attribution phenomenon. While an intentionally misleading communication deliberately attempts to conceal, involuntary deception manifests itself in terms of a number of factors based on equivocation and the absence of a context that causes confusion and misunderstanding.

With coercive persuasion, you can change the attitudes of people without them knowing about it without their knowledge. You can create new "attitudes" where they will do things willingly, things that they previously hated. Developments in the technologies of emotional stress generation and extreme anxiety, developments now at the very heart of coercive persuasion, surpass the old modes of coercion of a physical nature. The coercive persuasion changes as attitude and behavior. The coercive persuasion or thought reform is best understood as a coordinated system progressive coercive influence and behavioral control designed to deceive and surreptitiously manipulate and influence individuals, usually within a group.

The intensive use of interpersonal and psychological attacks to destabilize the subject's Self to promote obedience is based on:

- peer group use;
- the application of interpersonal pressure to promote standardization and compliance;
- the total manipulation of the social environment (by persons and/or places interposed - another person acting as an intermediary) of the individual to stabilize behaviors and attitudes of a modified faith.

Coercive persuasion speech is based on a fundamental fact: mystification (deceiving someone by distorting reality to make it more attractive, deceive someone by making fun of him, fooling around). It is a falsified speech whose purpose is not communication, but presents itself in the form of a perverse, one-way communication, almost of indoctrination. The strategy of mystification is to gradually move from the real to the illusory, without triggering a phenomenon of rejection. The mystification of speech is based on several elements:

a) Credibility: the speaker or author occupies a position of authority, real or fictional. Illustrated by Milgram's experiments, it is a question of obeying without reserve a recognized or proclaimed authority. Remember that to seduce is above all to please, but it is also to divert from the truth;

b) Fabulation (imaginary narrative presented as true): the persuasive discourse must disguise the real, mythologize it;

c) The Simulation (to give as real something that is not real): the speaker or the author plays, he creates an attractive character;

d) Concealment (adroitly avoid letting appear (one's thoughts, feelings, intentions), or seek to give a false idea): the speaker or the author masks his own interrogations, he hides his doubts;

e) Seduction (irresistibly pleasing, attracting someone irresistibly, captivating, speaking of something): the speaker or the author can not tell his story if it is not accompanied by the desire of the listener to hear until his denouement;

f) Contempt (Feeling of considering someone as worthless and not paying attention, not doing what one should normally do in a given situation, on a voluntary basis) : the persuader does not only disguise the reality through his speech, he also falsifies the relationship, thus establishing with the help of a perverse communication a relational dynamic perverse;

g) Persuasion: The process involves several

stages: attention, understanding, formatting, integration of the message, acceptance of the message, change of thought or attitude. The set is known by the acronym ELM (Elaboration Likelihood Model);

h) The Game Of The Persuader: the persuader has a double status. He is the sophist orator who convinces with an equivocal and ambiguous speech in lieu of answer and demonstration. He is also the mystifier who proposes dream and utopia as a set and costume in the theater of a collective illusion.

Coercive persuasion techniques:

1) ***Behavioral techniques:*** They consist of modifying the relations of the individual with his environment and aim to control the adept's exchanges with the previous relational system. They aim to modify the person's relationship with his environment and to control his exchanges: isolate him, control his information, weaken him and put him under dependence;

2) ***Emotional-type techniques:*** These techniques use emotional elicitation, a technique essentially aimed at provoking feelings and emotions in the subject;

a) to provoke fear and anxiety in her, for example by arbitrarily inflicting punishment on her, and

by randomly using leniency and severity;
b) to threaten it, because the promise of punishment, whether physical or psychological, is just as effective as the punishment itself;
c) make her feel guilty;

3) ***Cognitive-type techniques:*** The strategy consists of saturating its information channels with false data. At the same time, she will try to denigrate any critical attitude. These techniques are designed to confuse people with distortions of language and communication. Through the processes of perverse communication, one can engender doubt, confusion, shake the inner references and the good self-image of the other and prevent him from understanding what is happening to him. It is enough to multiply the contradictory or paradoxical messages, to lie, to refuse the direct communication, and to distort the language;

4) ***The techniques of induction of associative:*** states they create or recover pathological states (hallucinatory or delusions). It occurs in the victim physiological exhaustion, a renunciation to understand, a collapse of the critical capacity and automatic operation. DSM 4 (1996) states that dissociation may result from prolonged maneuvers of coercive persuasion. DSM-IV: dissociative amnesia, dissociative fugue, dissociative identity disorder, depersonalization disorder, and dissociative unspecified disorder. The hold can bring changes in

consciousness, a sort of imposed hypnotic state. The influence that the author exercises on his target diminishes his critical capacity and places it in a sort of trance that modifies his perceptions, sensations, and consciousness. This brings to her a vulnerability to suggestion and sometimes states of dissociation. Dissociation is an unconscious process whereby some thoughts are separated from the rest of the personality and function independently. The victim becomes an external observer of the aggression that she undergoes, it is a means of survival so as not to lose reason, a strategy when one has the feeling that there is no possible way out. Dissociative processes can lead people to "forget to remember" personal stressful events or even their entire past. In some cases, it is the opposite, people are invaded by the repetitive memories of aggression, think about it at any time, dream at night and all efforts to think of something else are in vain. These states can also induce a state of depersonalization with sensory anesthesia and a lack of emotional reaction or even a feeling of loss of control of his actions. Kihlstrom describes studies of various cognitive aspects in dissociative disorders such as autobiographical memory, episodic memory, and implicit memory. He is also interested in subclinical dissociation, which is characterized by dissociative manifestations that are insufficiently marked to be clinically significant, as well as medico-legal implications.

We know that when an individual learns by experience that he is incapable of acting on his environment to transform it into his favor (locus of control) when he becomes physiologically incapable of learning; we will talk about learned helplessness. This phenomenon was highlighted by Henri Laborit and studied by the neurobiologist Pierre Karli. This work was resumed in 1975 by Seligman, who described the concept of "learned helplessness ".

We can also speak of aversive conditioning or conditioning by aversion. The person is subjected to a set of artificial situations in a more or less controlled social environment whose objective is to introduce avoidance behaviors by an aversion to the subject. In clinical psychology, conditioning covers " all the associative operations by which we can provoke a new behavior in humans ". The learned helplessness occurs when the aggression is unpredictable and uncontrollable and there is no way to act to change the situation. Anticipation becomes impossible.

The first symptom of alienation is the loss by the individual of his own word and constitutes the essence of the process of personal development or that of the narcissistic function of the individual. The alienation is seen as the product of a breakdown in communication with oneself, breaking through which speech can no longer feed the unconscious.

The packaging invaded all fields of activity. It applies according to three complementary modes:

- cultural conditioning;
- emotional conditioning;
- fitness.

For conditioning to be operative, it is necessary to use a bundle of convergent techniques - physical and psychic. The coercive persuasion or thought reform or brainwashing is a process of indoctrination forced, which aims to reform the thought and to produce in the subject the desired behavior and attitude. These processes have reached a level of sophisticated and sophisticated sophistication and are based on recent theoretical advances in psychology, psychiatry, and neuropsychology, and are now used in the civil field. These processes are distinguished from crude, rudimentary, embryonic methods, or the processes were in the larval stage where the research was only beginning. To understand this, one must first have some knowledge about the psyche of beings and the functioning of consciousness, the transformations that are possible and the techniques used to achieve it. What looks like a magic trick is only the misleading application of the methods practiced.

Also, in this context, dependence is a consequence of grip and manipulation. Physiologically, it is a process by which behavior that can produce both pleasure and discards or alleviate a feeling of internal discomfort, is repeated without any control, although it is known that it is harmful, c is close to dependence on a psychoactive substance.

It is astonishing to see with what relative ease intelligent, autonomous, experienced people, who sometimes have heavy family or professional responsibilities, will suddenly be transformed into beings dependent on a new system of values and beliefs that shapes their whole mode of life. Becoming different beings, without even recognizing them themselves, they surprise their loved ones and move away, a little as if a barrier had fallen between them or they belonged to another world.

Coercive persuasion programs are effective because individuals experiencing the deliberately planned severe stresses that these programs generate. The relationship between the person and the tactics of coercive persuasion is dynamic and interactional in that the strength of the pressures, rewards, and punishments are considerable, and they do not lead to a stable, freely and significantly chosen reorganization of beliefs and attitudes. Rather, they lead to some sort of constrained submission and elaborate rationalization required for the new conduct.

The coercive persuasion or thought reform as it is sometimes called is best understood as a coordinated system of graduated coercive influence and behavior control designed to manipulate and influence deceptively and surreptitiously individuals, usually within a group.

In addition to using discourse and coercive persuasion techniques, hypnotic-type conditions can be established in different contexts using authority or peer group and manipulating the social environment of the subject:

- **Trust:** A person will be more open to suggestions if they trust the person making these suggestions. This confidence developed quietly throughout the approach work and then during the insertion into the group.
- **Expectations:** many promises are a way to create expectations. However, it is recognized that a prediction tends to be realized simply by believing in it. "The judicious use of expectations alone is enough to induce hypnosis because the subject's beliefs determine what will happen. "
- **Attitudes:** It takes a great deal of strength to resist the pressure of a peer group of believers. Differentiating among a group of "friends", colleagues, or interest group is not easy, especially when they have trapped our trust. To do this, verbal pressure is used, but also very often a form of disguised physical intimidation (close the person closely, make aggressive gestures, define it).
- **Motivations:** motivations, whether due to curiosity or the desire to experience the

promises made before, are an important factor. Well prepared psychologically by the group, this is the stage where the person wants to "go further".

The means the tactics of putting the conditions of mental manipulation into practice are simple and rely on the principle of the confusion, making the individual more manipulable:

The individual is prepared for thought reform by increasing suggestibility and/or "softening", specifically using hypnotic or suggestibility enhancing techniques such as (a) repetitive tactile or verbal exercises or having visual or audio elements; (b) routine activities involving excessive exact repetition; (c) a decrease in sleep; (d) nutritional restrictions.

Through the use of rewards and punishments, efforts are made to establish control over the social environment of the person, his time and the sources of his social support. Social isolation is promoted. Contacts with family and friends are abbreviated because they are contacts with people who do not share the group's attitudes. Economic dependency and others are maintained. (With the forerunner of coercive persuasion, it was rather easily accomplished by mere imprisonment.)

Communication is greatly controlled.

The absence of known landmarks. A person is more

easily influenced in a new place, away from home and those close to him.

Non-corroborating information and supporting opinions are prohibited or severely suppressed within the peer group's communication. Rules exist about permissible topics that can be discussed

Intense and frequent attempts are made to ensure that the person reassesses the most important aspects of his or her previous self-experience and negatively practices it. Efforts are designed to destabilize and undermine the subject's consciousness, a consciousness of reality, worldview, emotional control, and defense mechanisms as well as to reinterpret the story of his life. and adopt a new version of causality.

Intense and frequent attempts are made to shake the person into self-confidence and judgment, creating a feeling of helplessness.

Non-physical punishments are used such as, for example, intense humiliation, loss of privilege, social isolation, changes in social status, intense guilt, anxiety, manipulation and other techniques to create highly emotional dislikes, etc.

Some secular psychological [forces] are used or present: Failure to adopt the approved attitude, belief or behavior will lead to severe punishment or harsh consequences (eg, mental and physical illness, re-emergence of old physical illnesses, drug addiction, economic failures, social failures, divorces, disintegrations, failure to find a spouse, etc.).

- Disruption of metabolism by various strategies;
- Tiredness;

Recall that the principles of classical conditioning are at the basis of training and changing attitudes. In addition to triggering emotional responses, attitudes have a reinforcing and directive function. Attitudes have a central place in the analysis of social interaction where the person is a social stimulus for others, a stimulus that triggers positive or negative emotional responses, which has a reinforcing function and a directive function for approach or avoidance behaviors. In addition, the person's attitudes to herself, her self-concept, determine, in part, her behavior and the behavior of others in relation to herself. These are the principles that can guide the choice of intervention aimed at learning attitudes.

LEARN HOW TO OVERCOME MANIPULATION AND USE IT AGAINST THIS TYPE OF PEOPLE

Mentalism and seduction: the technique of invisible seduction

First of all, I would like to share with you one of my favorite quote on the theme of seduction, signed by a French novelist Jules Barbey d'Aurevilly :

> "The supreme seduction is not to express one's feelings. This is to make them suspect. "

The tools of mentalism can greatly increase the charisma and overcome his fears (fear of seduction approach, defeat his phobias and so on). What is very interesting in the approach of seduction by mentalism is that it allows creating an unconscious grip. Mentalism reveals what is happening unconsciously in our head.

What interests us is this unconscious approach; that is to say the invisible seduction.

What is "invisible seduction"?

It is a subtle seduction that uses:

- Non-verbal language: your attitude, your actions.
- Para-verbal language: the tone of your voice, the intonation, and the rhythm.
- The verbal: the spread, use of storytellings, metaphors, and humor.

In this section, we will mainly talk about seduction for men.

Finally, invisible seduction does not give the woman the sensation that you are seducing her and yet this book is not exhaustive but explains 7 essential keys that will allow you to create the connection with the person you want to seduce.

To seduce is to create Attraction

The attraction is simply an attraction. Without attraction, there is no desire, no connection, and no seduction. When I speak of attraction, I am NOT talking about physical attraction but spiritual attraction, one that creates a positive reaction in the minds of others, that little inner voice that whispers to him: "This man is special ... I appreciate his company, he seems to understand me, to be like me. "

1st key: Humor!

This is most certainly the most important to create the report. From the beginning, humor creates a link with the other. In situations of seduction, we will mainly use teasing. It's charming humor! To tease, just use derision and especially ... self-mockery. In seduction, never take yourself seriously. If she stammers, if you stumble, if she has a special laugh, tease her.

Teasing is of course NON-AGGRESSIVE. Not everyone is sensitive to this ... although I must admit that 80% of the time, it works. There are of course other keys, here they are.

2nd key: Create The Report!

The bond is created when one feels good with the other. Humor is the first step. The second, as I discuss in my book, is "Anecdotes, Exchange and Interest." To seduce a person, it is important to really know his passions, his interests, what drives him. To interest someone, as I told you in the section on the art of making friends, is to talk about them.

• Start finding topics that interest him. Example: Evenings, clothing tastes ...

• Amplify: enter deeper into the topic of conversation.

This step is not about starting a series of questions and answers. CAREFULLY listen to his answers. This will allow you to enter new frames, i.e. find new topics of conversation.

Of course, it may be that some conversations lead to nothing, here comes the famous white. You then have several possibilities to get out of it:

• Talk about yourself: "Personally, this is the first time I come here, I was expecting (...)"

• Change the subject: Use the environment, the context, the previous topics that animated the debate

• Leave to come back: The environment is, of course, to take into account, if you are several, you can leave to reopen the conversation later.

3rd key: Manage The Barriers!

Women like to test men. Moreover, it is a way to selectmen likely to seduce ... "We know each other? " "You're too young for me ..." etc. How to react to these test questions?

• NEVER show that it destabilizes you.

• Answer in a fun way, turn it against her.

"Do we know each other?" Answer: "Of course not, I have not asked you for your name yet."

To seduce is to create comfort. You have 3 keys for the moment, these allow you to create the interest. After that, the goal is to deepen and make the relationship comfortable, enjoyable. You are no longer the unknown, but do not stop creating attraction ... On the contrary.

4th key: The Art Of Detachment!

Being detached simply gives the image of a man sure of him. This could be our main key.

• Work on your non-verbal gestures: Make quiet gestures, be relaxed, sure of yourself. Do not give too much sensation that your "body belongs to the other". The idea is simple: Do not turn entirely towards the other, synchronize yourself with the posture of your partner. Be "free in your environment", you do not belong to anyone.

• The attraction-repulsion: More commonly called the "push-pull", this strategy is to give interest to the other than completely stop giving it! Talk to people, expand your social circle and come back to each other. Just like verbal language, your attitude with the woman you want to seduce must demonstrate some quiet strength.

• Silence your little negative inner voice. The main concern in seduction comes from the negative thoughts that assail us: "She does not want me"; "She finds me heavy and so on ..." Shut up these thoughts, and act positively.

- Smile! Instead of asking questions, learn to be cool and open. It's terribly attractive, and it makes the relationship very comfortable.

5th key: Similarities, Oppositions And Future.

The similarities make it possible to create attraction and comfort ... But the oppositions too! The oppositions allow to:

- Demonstrate great strength of character.

- Demonstrate to the woman that you are a man who will be able to oppose if necessary.

- Tease!

    ⇨ "Do you like country music? I thought you were great and there ... Everything collapses! (Humorous) Explain to me why! "

Play these oppositions too, and you will gain the respect and interest of the woman. It's something that I wanted to highlight in my book, it's very important! Just like the time distortion, which consists of talking about the future ... Women like to imagine, to feel, to see the future ("You like extreme sports ... Super ... We parachute when you want ...").

Create opportunities, give the feeling that you want to consider things in the future with her. "I am the champion in board games! How do you think you can beat me? See you next Wednesday ... ".

You can stay fun, the goal is to suggest the future ... Seduce is to create sexual tension! Of course, sex plays a role in the process of seduction. To conclude seduction is necessary to go through sex.

6th key: Physical Contact

This physical contact must be initiated early in a relationship, it has a real impact on the unconscious. When you tease, you (must) can touch the person. The more the report is done, the more you will see a physical connection. So we do not talk purely about sex, but it helps a lot to be intimate with the person.

7th key: Intimacy

When you find yourself alone with the person, sex is no longer really a hypothesis. It is (if you have of course followed the process of seduction) an obviousness. There may, however, be resistance, but you have managed to create enough attraction and install a relationship of comfort.

HOW TO USE SUBLIMINAL MESSAGES TO PERSUADE PEOPLE IN AN UNDETECTED WAY

Hidden persuaders: the psychology of subliminal perception

Nearly fifty years ago, an American writer named Packard argued that by using subliminal cues, advertisers and sellers persuaded people to buy against their will. They were being cynically manipulated. The theory is that people can be emotionally and behaviorally affected by visual or vocal stimuli whose presence they do not report.

Whether it is preconscious processing of unconscious perception, few psychologists argue or even be surprised by the idea that people can be affected by stimuli they claim they have not seen. What people say they saw and saw is not the same.

By updating images and words very quickly, scientists have been able to reliably demonstrate the process called subliminal perception. But it is very large, but there is very little evidence that subliminal perception systematically and consistently influences a person's attitudes, beliefs, choices, and motives. There is, in summary, little or no reliable scientific evidence that subliminal perception has any impact on behavior or a long-term effect on consumer intentions or behavior.

But the lack of evidence never got in the way of a good theory. So over the years, journalists and popular authors have argued that some, even most ads contain hidden sexual images or brand names or particular messages that affect our susceptibility to those ads. So the flashy, paranoid, but test-free myth goes: smart (evil) advertisers can make you do things against your best judgment, conscious decision or will, through subliminal messages in advertisements (mainly on television, but also on the radio). A careful investigation has suggested, as one critic put it: this idea is absurd or laughable and ridiculous, paranoid and absurd.

5 steps to launch a new life

- A simple cure for impulsive excessive spending
- Do you have a mental model of external validation?
- Experts answer some common questions about common divorce
- An averaging bias
- Conspiracy theories always make a good copy. We have gone from Big Brother, 1984 type conspiracy to commercial conspiracy. The big

companies, attended by audacious foreign capitalists, are abusing us without mercy, especially the naive and credulous. They supposedly have the power to turn us into mannequins and puppets.

We know that advertisements use words or visual or vocal themes to encourage us to establish connections between brands, products, and particular behaviors and emotions. We also know that ads can influence attitudes and values without the awareness of people. But this is not subliminal advertising.

From the late 1950s to the mid-1970s, books with titles like Subliminal Seduction and Media Sexploitation kept the notion alive for an apparently happy audience to see the evil manipulative scientists working with greedy and cynical advertisers. Alcoholism, suicides and sexual disorders were considered partly consequences of this conspiracy.

But smart sellers saw the positive side of the public's credulity. They knew from their research that subliminal advertising did not work ... and somehow it was illegal and illogical. But why not change everything and openly sell the technique? Ready! We have subliminal audio self - help tapes.

Soon tapes were sold that supposedly showed dramatic changes in mental and psychological health. Simply set the recorder to turn off while you sleep and you may experience weight loss, improved sexual function, and ease of quitting, biting your nails or fear of flying. The tapes came in several forms. Some were designed to be played while awake. But they all had those embedded subliminal messages that you could not understand but that could change your life.

Then the modality changed from visual to auditory and the image of the science of impious to useful. The scientists went to work on this, testing the claim that an undetectable voice signal changes behavior. It is a stronger claim than if the critical messages are masked (choked or disappear) by other sounds, the weak is detected, then unraveled and then it is understandable.

The ribbons provide a pipe to the Id: that Freudian concept of the primitive person that is a cauldron of boiling excitement. It can, they say, reach the deepest parts of our being.

But scientists have tested these assumptions carefully. The jury has returned. There is no evidence for most of these theoretically confusing statements. Therefore, this is not just quackery but a fraud: the ads have the obvious intention of deceiving people who want a quick and cheap "cure" that involves little willpower or pain.

And here is the paradox. Scientific evidence is often full of warnings and is not written in every day, easily accessible language. The scientists write to each other.

Scientists could be unanimous in their opinion based on the evidence that subliminal tapes make fraudulent claims, but they do not seem too hot to convey their message.

On the other hand, producers of tapes with commercial experience have commissioned advertising agencies to design new campaigns. Using scientific jargon and images and the power of repetition, aggressive campaigns have succeeded in keeping the myths alive. It is ironic that traditional advertising manages to sell subliminal tapes that do not convince.

Advertisers and marketing people are smart and resourceful. They know how to manipulate our mood that can influence our behavior while shopping. They do everything possible to make us remember their brand and have positive associations with it. And now they are turning to " brain science " to make them even more successful. The hope for many is to find those "hidden persuaders" that can actually work this time.

Subliminal messages and manipulation

What is a subliminal message? It is a message (video, sound or pictographic) that is perceived by the senses and analyzed by the brain but is not communicated to the consciousness. For example, a video game distills loudspeakers in the loudspeakers that sound like compliments but whose intensity is so low that the player does not hear them. And although the player is not aware, these messages influence the brain since it analyzes them all the same and also satisfies the ego of the player who is more and more happy to play a game yet stupid.

Researchers Sheng He and Donald McLeod report in Nature (May 24, 2001) an experiment of the same kind. They projected with a laser on the retina of subjects, parallel lines so close that the subjects could distinguish only an even block of color. But when the experimenters showed them more distant lines, the guinea pigs remained undecided long enough to answer. In this experiment, the retina always distinguished the lines even very close together. It turns out that it is the visual cortex that decides whether to pass on the information to the rest of the brain. But according to what selection criteria, we do not know yet.

Similarly, in a movie (succession of 24 frames per second), if you drag an image that has nothing to do with the current sequence (e.g. an advertisement), a spectator could not realize it consciously because of the speed of scrolling. While the image is yet detected by the eye cells and sent to the visual cortex. This image and its semantic content are analyzed by the brain but are not taken into account by the mechanisms of consciousness that ignore it at the moment it is perceived. On the other hand, the information contained in this image can possibly influence the behavior of the spectator.

Other techniques consist in superimposing on an image or a video, another quasi-transparent image; or to integrate a subliminal image into a fast trajectory object across the screen. Another example: currently, in a film channel, the video sequence presenting an animated logo of the advertiser that manages the advertising space that is broadcast before each film; presents brand names almost imperceptible since it scrolls at a very fast pace with special effects that integrate them into a setting that almost hides our consciousness. But if you pay attention, you can still see them. You can also "hide" in a musical piece a sound message of lower intensity and so on.

It is to be feared that advertisers and commercials use this type of method without our knowledge to consume us. Moreover, this problem concerns all media: radio, posters, video games, movies, TV series, TV news, etc. It would be dangerous to let anyone deprive us of our free will by subliminal messages whose purpose is not elsewhere not always commercial.

How to detect subliminal messages?

The use of subliminal messages in experiments and therapies has been practiced since the 1860s. Later, it was used in advertising. Although most people are not aware of the use and effectiveness of these messages and may even consider suggesting that they are used in the field of "science fiction" or "fantasy", some researchers have spent years studying these methods to "secretly" influence the processes of human thought and therefore behavior. The detection and decoding of subliminal messages begin with the study of printed advertisements in search of hidden images or perceptual ambiguities that are imperceptible without targeted concentration.

Study the content of ads, images, and words, and determine if something seems out of place or rare (like advertising elements and their location), or hidden in the background or in an image (use the magnifying glass for a more detailed study). Determines whether the ad is a photo or a real representation of an artist. Write down your observations.

Answer the following questions about the ad, as Bill Chapman suggests in his "Classroom Tools":

- Who is it for?
- Is it commercial or non-commercial?
- In a clear and brief sentence, how would you summarize the message?

- Are there any other messages in this element? does the author try to provoke a behavior or a belief?
- What is the behavior or belief that the author expects of the target?
- Does the message attempt to manipulate with emotion, reason, or both?
- How do you think the manipulation works?
- According to you, this section has succeeded in propaganda?
- What evidence supports your answer?

Choose print ads that advertise products for exercise or weight loss. Answer the same questions as in Step 2 to determine which subliminal messages, if any, are used to sell the product.

Advice

Learning to detect and decipher subliminal messages requires the practice and deliberate study of the elements of an advertisement to determine what lies beneath the surface. Raising awareness that an advertisement in any medium is often a sophisticated attempt to convince the viewer to buy or use a particular product can also help explain why a person is particularly attracted to one product or another.

Warnings

After seeing how advertising uses subliminal messages to encourage destructive behavior, we may think that all subliminal messages are bad or even harmful. The student of the subliminal messages should realize that their use can also be used to encourage positive behaviors through the use of positive subliminal affirmations and self-hypnosis. Using subliminal messages in this way can correct destructive behaviors, create a positive self-image and reinforce constructive behaviors.

CONCLUSION

Do most of us really try to manipulate other people to get our own way? Even just from time to time and not being obvious about it? One consideration is the theory that we each have a natural tendency towards self-orientation. An inclination that can result in selfishness.

Just as well you might say, for how else can we survive in this competitive world? However, the usual spiritual perspective is to bear in mind the needs of others: not prioritizing self but balancing one's own wants with those of others. Perhaps we might ask ourselves this question. Is there a danger in making self-orientation the chief of our motives. In other words, having a self-concern that is over and above consideration for the rights of others?

It seems to follow that when self-orientation rules then we always want to get our own way, to win the argument and be seen to be in the right, to feel superior to others and dominate them. Is such an attitude not shown by wanting to manipulate someone so we gain control for the sake of self-interest?

The bad news is that being manipulative can only result in poor personal relationships. This means we would miss out on the chance of a union of mutual respect and care.

Applying all you have learned in this book should be done with extreme caution.

www.ingramcontent.com/pod-product-compliance
Lightning Source LLC
Chambersburg PA
CBHW070906080526
44589CB00013B/1194